TEEN
SERVICES 101

A Practical Guide for
Busy Library Staff

MEGAN P. FINK

Contents

Introduction

ACCORDING TO THE Public Library Association's 2012 "PLDS Statistical Report," only 33% of public libraries employ at least one full-time teen services librarian. What this means is that the majority of librarians and library staff currently serving teens in public libraries are not specifically trained to work with teens and may not have ever planned to work with teens. In smaller libraries especially, teen services may be performed by children's services librarians, adult services librarians, or non-librarian staff, who may find dealing with teens an unfamiliar and daunting experience. In addition, a report from the Institute of Museum and Library Services (IMLS) noted that 77% of all public libraries are small, with a median staff of 2.5 FTE, and 47% of all public libraries are rural, with a median staff of 1.5 FTE. So there are many libraries out there that would like to do more for teens in their community, but that struggle finding the time and resources to achieve this goal. If any of this describes you—you didn't expect to work with teenagers, your previous work experience is with other age groups, your coursework didn't focus on teen services, you're busy with other responsibilities—then you're reading the right book!

While serving teens has its own challenges, incorporating or increasing services to this age group can have incredible benefits for your library. Teens can provide volunteer services and word-of-mouth advertising for library programs. Teen programming can increase the visibility of your library in the local community. And, perhaps most importantly, incorporating teens in the life of your library sets up future library supporters. Successful brands know to cultivate the loyalty of children and teenagers in order to build a body of loyal adult customers. The teen library patrons of today will become the adult taxpayers of the future, and if they have positive experiences with your library, they will be more likely to support it when library funding comes up for a vote.

In addition to benefiting your library, working with teens can also have benefits for you in your professional life. Teens are often early adopters of new technologies, as well as initiators of new trends, and teens can help you keep up with developments before they become mainstream among adults. Developing events for teens encourages creative, out-of-the-box thinking that can be applied to events for adults or children and can keep things fresh and interesting. Working with teens also offers library staff a chance to mentor in a way that working with adults or children does not—an experience that can be extremely rewarding!

According to the YALSA report *The Future of Library Services for and with Teens: A Call to Action*, there are four essential goals for libraries and teens:

- Bridge the Growing Digital and Knowledge Divide: School and public libraries must ensure that in addition to providing access to digital tools, they also provide formal and informal opportunities for teens to learn to use these tools in meaningful and authentic ways.
- Build on Teens' Motivation to Learn: Too often teens' desire to learn is thwarted by an educational system too focused on testing, unwilling to adopt culturally relevant pedagogy, or so strapped for funding that only basic resources are available. Libraries live outside of a school's formal academic achievement sphere and offer a space where interest-based learning can occur in a risk-free environment. Public and school libraries, therefore, need to embrace their role as both formal and informal learning spaces.
- Provide Workforce Development Training: In order to address the growing need for a skilled workforce, school and public libraries have the responsibility to enable teens to learn in relevant, real-world twenty-first-century contexts.
- Serve as the Connector between Teens and Other Community Agencies: Libraries are only one of many organizations with a vision to build better futures for teens. Too often, however, teens are unaware of the services offered in their communities. As many

of today's teens are faced with serious social and economic challenges, libraries must provide teens the assistance they need.[1]

Serving teens is an essential need that can benefit libraries that embrace this opportunity and partner with community organizations to provide education on job-related skills to teens. "With over 40 million adolescents, aged 12–17, living in the United States today . . . a 2013 Pew survey found that 72% of 16- to 17-year-olds had used a public library in 2012."[2]

HOW TO READ THIS BOOK

This book is divided into eight chapters based on the general job requirements of working for and with teens. Most chapters, while they do contain useful background information, focus on the practical concerns of day-to-day life on the job. To help you with your work, this book contains many lists, checklists, anecdotes, and examples. Feel free to skip directly to those in the sidebars and Works Cited lists, if they will help you the most. This book does not have to be read from start to finish— feel free to skip from chapter to chapter depending on your needs. You may also want to skip ahead to the appendixes, which contain some extremely useful websites and ideas for further exploration.

CHAPTER SUMMARIES

1. Why Teen Services?

Libraries that offer services for teens provide more value to their community and position themselves to become a critical resource that garners widespread community support. In this first chapter you will find:

---

1. Linda W. Braun, Maureen L. Hartman, Sandra Hughes-Hassell, and Kafi Kumasi, with contributions from Beth Yoke, *The Future of Library Services for and with Teens: A Call to Action*, January 8, 2014, http://www.ala.org/yaforum/sites/ala.org.yaforum/files/content/YALSA_nationalforum_final.pdf.
2. Braun et al., *Future of Library Services*.

- Statistics on the benefits for libraries of offering teen programming.
- Anecdotes from librarians and library workers who have implemented teen programs and seen a difference in their library.

2. Successfully Managing Teen Behavior for the Benefit of All

Teenagers do not always think or behave like adults, and for a good reason: teenagers are undergoing massive developmental changes, both physically and neurologically. This chapter will discuss the effect that the changing teenage brain can have on teen behavior, and how a library worker can take this into account when interacting with teen patrons.

- A quick guide to teen brain development.
- Step-by-step techniques for managing challenging behavior.

3. Developing the Teen Collection

Now more than ever, libraries play an important role in curating the vast amount of information that is available to the public, including teens. This chapter will provide resources for developing a basic but solid teen collection, whether growing and revitalizing an existing collection or starting from scratch. The variety of materials available for teens—graphic novels and manga, e-books and apps, nonfiction and periodicals—will be touched on, as will collection analysis and trend spotting. It discusses:

- How to spot what's popular among teens in your community.
- The top four resources for collection development.
- A four-step plan for building a teen collection from scratch.

4. Making a Welcoming Space for Teens

Just as not all libraries have a teen services librarian, not all have a designated teen space. This chapter will provide strategies for making sure a library is teen-friendly and, when possible, carving out some space for teens in those libraries that do not yet have a teen space. This chapter will also provide some basic resources for those libraries that do have a designated teen space, including how to develop fair and appropriate policies governing teen spaces, and resources to consult when developing a teen space. The importance of teen ownership and involvement in planning and managing teen spaces will also be explored. The chapter provides:

- Resources for designing your teen space.
- Real-life before-and-after examples of teen spaces.
- Sample policies and rules for teen spaces.

5. Programming

Libraries need to offer a basic core of teen programs in order to help their community's teens succeed in school and prepare for college and careers. This chapter will cover resources for program inspiration and ideas for inexpensive and easy-to-run programs, as well as methods to market and promote teen library programs. Different ways to involve teens in program planning and implementation will also be explored. This chapter will contain a special section on Teen Summer Reading/Learning:

- Programs-in-a-Box: plans and supply lists for popular, simple programs.
- Planning a Teen Summer Reading/Learning Program: the bare bones list, including ideas for activities, incentives, marketing, and design.

6. Leveraging Teen Volunteers and Teen Advisory Boards to Boost Your Capacity

Developing a core group of volunteer workers can help library staff achieve more and make their job easier. Additionally, volunteering not only provides teens with valuable opportunities to develop creativity and leadership skills; it can also be a great way to cultivate a positive relationship between the library and teens in the community. This chapter will discuss the management of teen volunteers, forming a teen volunteer group, curating existing groups, and effectively managing solo volunteers, and covers:

- Sample volunteer applications and policies.
- What can your volunteers do for you? Examples of simple, recurring tasks that volunteers can take off your hands.
- A guide to training volunteers and preventing common problems.

7. Providing Virtual Library Services to Help Teens (& You) 24/7

Technology, especially social media and mobile technology, can be an easy way for librarians and library workers to deliver fast and free services to teens. This chapter will explore many ways that librarians and library workers can use technology to reach and serve teens, including using social media to communicate with teens, soliciting and incorporating teen-created content online, and integrating mobile technology into library services. It also includes:

- A guide to using social media platform to interact with teen patrons.
- How to get started with social media—even if you've never run a social media page before.
- Guidelines for integrating mobile technology into your library.

8. Increasing Your Impact with Community Partnerships

One of the functions of libraries is to connect different groups of people in the community. Community partnerships can also make serving teens easier and less expensive for the library. Whether utilizing the local school librarians' network or communicating with local businesses, this chapter will discuss how to create relationships in your community to more effectively serve teens and to increase your impact, including:

- Real-life examples of successful community partnerships.
- How to create and maintain fruitful partnerships.
- A guide to managing projects with partners.

APPENDICES

Many relevant YALSA resources are referenced throughout the text. The appendixes contain lists of these resources for easy reference.

A. YALSA's Competencies for Librarians Serving Youth: Young Adults Deserve the Best
B. Teen Space Guidelines
C. Teen Programming Guidelines – Draft

1 | Why Teen Services?

LIBRARIES THAT OFFER services for and with teens provide more value to their community and position themselves to become a critical resource that garners widespread community support. This chapter includes the following:

- Statistics on the benefits for libraries of offering teen programming.
- Anecdotes from librarians and library workers who have implemented teen programs and seen a difference in their library.

> "Libraries are about freedom. Freedom to read, freedom of ideas, freedom of communication. They are about education (which is not a process that finishes the day we leave school or university), about entertainment, about making safe spaces, and about access to information."
>
> —Neil Gaiman

BENEFITS OF TEEN PROGRAMMING

A teen-friendly library provides an affinity group for teens in your community who are seeking an outlet for knowledge, entertainment, and the pursuit of reading. As J. K. Rowling, the author of the Harry Potter series, wrote: "When in doubt, go to the library."[1] The effect of teen ser-

---

1. "J. K. Rowling Quotes," *Good Reads*, http://www.goodreads.com/quotes/223272-when-in-doubt-go-to-the-library.

vices on a community is measurable in the quality of programming and the collection that are offered to teen patrons. Libraries provide equal-opportunity access to technology, books, and mentoring regardless of socioeconomic background. And the number of children and young adults using public libraries is steadily increasing every year.[2] In addition to advocating a lifelong love of reading, libraries also nurture the academic and digital-literacy skills that teens will use in future careers. According to the 2013 Pew Study "Younger Americans' Library Habits and Experiences," the popularity of books is continuing in addition to the growing prevalence of e-books. In addition, the report cites the following statistics:

- 65% of Americans ages 16–29 have a library card.
- 75% of younger Americans say they have read at least one book in print in the past year, compared with 64% of adults ages 30 and older.
- 60% of younger patrons say they go to the library to study, sit and read, or watch or listen to media.
- 80% of Americans under age 30 say that librarians are a "very important" resource for libraries to have.[3]

Libraries can also serve as a community center for teens to spend time with adult mentors and friends in a safe place. The multiple valuable facets of a teen-friendly library as a source for information, socialization, and recreation are recognized by teenagers in the United States. According to the 2007 Harris Interactive poll "American Library Association Youth and Library Use Study": "Thirty-one percent [of teens] visit the public library more than ten times a year and nearly 70% use their school library more than once a month."[4] Libraries that are teen-friendly

2. Kathryn Zickuhr et al., "Young Americans' Library Habits and Expectations," *Pew Internet*, June 25, 2013, http://libraries.pewinternet.org/2013/06/25/younger-americans-library-services/.
3. Zickuhr et al., "Young Americans' Library Habits."
4. Harris Interactive, "American Library Association Youth and Library Use Study," June 2007, http://www.ala.org/yalsa/sites/ala.org.yalsa/files/content/professionaltools/HarrisYouthPoll.pdf.

provide a community feature that encourages teens to seek out information from the information experts: librarians. According to the Pew Study "Younger Americans' Library Habits and Expectations," teens rely on libraries in their areas for online access:

- "Some 38% of Americans ages 16–29 have used computers and the internet at libraries in the past year, compared with 22% of those ages 30 and older. Among those who use computers and internet at libraries, young patrons are more likely than older users to use the library's computers or internet to do research for school or work, visit social networking sites, or download or watch online video."
- 84% of Americans ages 16 and older have ever visited a library or bookmobile in person.[5]

With teenagers' desire for online access and their reliance on technology for social and work-related skills, libraries provide a valuable resource. According to the YALSA report *The Future of Library Services for and with Teens: A Call to Action,* "More than 81% of online teens use some kind of social media, and texting dominates their general communication choices."[6] The socioeconomic technology divide means that students need a free resource that will fill in the gaps and provide both access to current technologies and opportunities for building digital-literacy skills. In order to create lifelong readers, library staff need to create compelling programming and encourage teens to experience a variety of genres and reading modalities. The need for a literate, informed population is one of the foundations of the United States' democratic society. "Only one method of improving reading ability really works: engaging in a great deal of interesting (better yet, compelling), comprehensible reading. Massive evidence supports this view, both in first and second

5. Zickuhr et al., "Young Americans' Library Habits."
6. Linda W. Braun, Maureen L. Hartman, Sandra Hughes-Hassell, and Kafi Kumasi, with contributions from Beth Yoke, *The Future of Library Services for and with Teens: A Call to Action,* January 8, 2014, http://www.ala.org/yaforum/sites/ala.org.yaforum/files/content/YALSA_nationalforum_final.pdf.

language research. Briefly, studies show that those who read more read better. They also write better, spell better, have larger vocabularies, and have better control of complex grammatical constructions."[7]

Libraries bridge the digital divide by providing free, equal access to computers, the Internet, and technology for teens. According to the American Library Association's website, "In a 2007 poll, it was found that one-third of teens between the ages of 12–18 visited the public library ten times a year or more."[8] Whether for free online access or for help with research, libraries provide a safe place for teens to socialize and seek information. Since reading is a lifelong skill connected to the ability to interpret, analyze, and synthesize information, libraries are the essential tools for teenagers to enhance their education. According to the American Association of School Librarians (AASL), "Reading is a foundational skill for learning, personal growth, and enjoyment. The degree to which students can read and understand text in all formats (e.g., pictures, video, print) and all contexts is a key indicator of success in school and in life. As a lifelong learning skill, reading goes beyond decoding and comprehension to interpretation and development of new understandings."[9] These new understandings include digital reading; all teens are not prepared equally and rely on librarian and library workers for assistance. As YALSA's *Future of Library Services for and with Teens* report states:

> *Perhaps more important is the need for public and school libraries to address what Dave Lankes calls the "knowledge gap"—"the ability of people to take advantage of these new tools." Digital-literacy skills are critical for completing homework, applying for a job, accessing government online resources, applying to college, being successful in the work-force, contributing to the democratic process, communicating*

7. Stephen Krashen, "Anything but Reading," *Knowledge Quest* 37, no. 5 (May/June 2009).
8. ALA, ed., "Teens 13–18 Quick Facts and Statistics," *American Library Association Advocacy*, 2014, http://www.ala.org/advocacy/advleg/advocacyuniversity/additup/13to18/quick.
9. ALA, "Teens 13–18 Quick Facts."

with peers—the list goes on. While teens are often referred to as "digital natives," research shows that many teens are no more savvy about technology, digital media, or the web than adults. Thus, school and public libraries must ensure that in addition to providing access to the tools, that they also provide formal and informal opportunities for teens to learn to use them in meaningful and authentic ways. Closing the knowledge gap is a critical goal of library staff.[10]

In addition to developing reading and technology skills, libraries create a community for teens to socialize in and build key soft skills, such as teamwork, conflict management, self-confidence, accepting constructive criticism, and more. According to the State of America's Libraries research, "Among Americans ages 16 years and older, 80% say borrowing books is a 'very important' service libraries provide, and 80% say reference librarians fall into the same 'very important' category. Free access to computers and the internet finished in a virtual tie, at 77%."[11] YALSA's *The Future of Library Services for and with Teens* report suggests that a teen-friendly library can garner wide influence in its community by improving teenagers' success in school, enhancing their career and college readiness, and helping close the information literacy gap by using connected learning. Indeed, librarians and library workers interact with teenagers by teaching literacy skills "under a larger umbrella of multiple literacies, which encompasses information literacies, critical literacies, digital literacies, media literacies, and much more."[12] These skills relate to social engagement, community connection, sharing and expressing knowledge in various formats, and learning how to use technology ethically and responsibly.

Author Neil Gaiman writes about the importance of libraries in his life and the leadership and inspiration that librarians and library staff provided during his childhood:

---

10. Braun et al., *Future of Library Services.*
11. ALA, *State of America's Libraries Report 2013 Public Libraries*, 2014, http://www. ala.org/news/state-americas-libraries-report-2013/public-libraries.
12. Braun et al., *Future of Library Services.*

They were good librarians. They liked books and they liked the books being read. They taught me how to order books from other libraries on inter-library loans. They had no snobbery about anything I read. They just seemed to like that there was this wide-eyed little boy who loved to read, and would talk to me about the books I was reading, they would find me other books in a series, they would help. They treated me as another reader—nothing less or more—which meant they treated me with respect. I was not used to being treated with respect as an eight-year-old. But libraries are about freedom. Freedom to read, freedom of ideas, freedom of communication. They are about education (which is not a process that finishes the day we leave school or university), about entertainment, about making safe spaces, and about access to information.[13]

This encounter of respect, freedom, and initiation into a world of reading for pleasure is the essential creed of libraries.

According to Gaiman, the rate of information created in the twenty-first century requires library staff to help navigate the multifaceted options. Gaiman states, "In the last few years, we've moved from an information-scarce economy to one driven by an information glut. According to Eric Schmidt of Google, every two days now the human race creates as much information as we did from the dawn of civilization until 2003. That's about five exobytes of data a day, for those of you keeping score. The challenge becomes, not finding that scarce plant growing in the desert, but finding a specific plant growing in a jungle. We are going to need help navigating that information to find the thing we actually need."[14] The teen-friendly library creates such a tool to find information by developing a teen-centered environment with online access and knowledgeable staff who are enthusiastic about serving teens.

---

13. Neil Gaiman, "Why Our Future Depends on Libraries, Reading and Daydreaming," *Guardian*, October 15, 2013, http://www.theguardian.com/books/2013/oct/15/neil-gaiman-future-libraries-reading-daydreaming.
14. Gaiman, "Why Our Future Depends on Libraries."

The socioeconomic equalizer provided by libraries is another valuable asset to our communities. As Gaiman posits:

> *Libraries are places that people go to for information. Books are only the tip of the information iceberg: they are there, and libraries can provide you freely and legally with books. More children are borrowing books from libraries than ever before—books of all kinds: paper and digital and audio. But libraries are also, for example, places that people, who may not have computers, who may not have internet connections, can go online without paying anything: hugely important when the way you find out about jobs, apply for jobs or apply for benefits is increasingly migrating exclusively online. Librarians can help these people navigate that world.*[15]

Creating a welcoming environment is one of the responsibilities of librarians and library workers. According to a recent survey in the journal *Young Adult Library Services (YALS)*, teens remember library staff who take the time to get to know them and who can relate to their personal interests, such as the "little details that count like remembering names, where they go to school, what courses they take, what books they took out the last time."[16]

Summer reading and learning to avoid the summer slide is another avenue for teen-friendly libraries to provide more value to their community. According to a recent Pew Research Center survey on library usage, teens are "significantly more likely than those [people] ages 30 and older to use the library as a study or 'hang out' space."[17] Teens need an opportunity to avoid the summer slide of academics and engage in creative programming at the public library. The experience of self-selecting books

15. Gaiman, "Why Our Future Depends on Libraries."
16. Rachel Randall, "All Wired Up: Understanding the Reading and Information Searching Behaviors of Teenagers," *YALS* (Summer 2013): 19–22.
17. Eugenia Williamson, "New Breed of Teen Services Librarians Emerges," *Boston Globe*, October 11, 2013, http://www.bostonglobe.com/lifestyle/2013/10/11/new-breed-teen-services-librarians-emerges/mybVRaDDY2mPgezrxMWSmN/story.html.

and having a successful reading experience is a valuable community service of public libraries. According to the New York State Library:

> *In their studies of children's reading development, McGill-Franzen and Allington (2003) cite the importance of extensive, successful reading experiences in the development of reading proficiency. If children have the opportunity to listen to, discuss, and read books on topics that they select, they will develop extensive background information which can serve as a platform from which to engage in their own independent reading. Additional studies by Guthrie and Anderson (1999) found that "a history of less-successful reading experiences produces a lessened interest in voluntary reading than a history of successful reading experiences." According to Cunningham and Stanovich (1998), the key predictors of positive reading development are success when learning to read and numerous opportunities and experiences with reading. Children who enjoy reading will read more and become proficient at the same time. A report from the National Institute of Education (1988) concluded that "the amount of reading done out of school is consistently related to gains in reading achievement."* [18]

Summer slide extends beyond loss in reading and literacy skills to math skills as well. Libraries can help ensure that teens do not lose the skills they gained during the school year by offering a range of learning opportunities during the summer. More and more libraries are leveraging resources from organizations, such as the National Summer Learning Association, and incorporating STEM-focused (science, technology, engineering, math) activities into their summer reading/learning programs in order to prevent all aspects of the summer slide.

---

18. New York State Library, "The Importance of Summer Reading," NYSED.gov, April 24, 2013, http://www.nysl.nysed.gov/libdev/summer/research.htm.

E-BOOKS AND READING EXPERIENCES

As more children gain experiences of reading through e-books and tablet devices, they will expect libraries to complement those interests in their library collections of e-books and devices. According to a 2014 study from the *Digital Shift* journal, e-books enhance a child's literacy experience.[19] In the 2014 study, children were given iPads, iPods, and a touch-screen computer in reading sessions, and "the authors speculate that the 'spatial and temporal synchrony' of children looking, listening, *and* touching while reading may be the 'sweet spot' that garners their 'attention to e-text in ways that support early literacy experience and learning.'"[20] Teen-friendly libraries are the next progression for this digitized generation that will be drawn to e-books and will expect a library that is equipped to feed their e-readers. In fact, 32% of respondents in the "Young Americans' Library Habits and Expectations" study by the Pew Research Center said they would be likely to use e-readers loaded with e-books.[21]

Furthermore, teen-friendly libraries cultivate an educational environment that can assist teenagers with their homework and improve their literacy skills. Students will need experience researching online, and librarians are equipped to help them hone their critical reading skills. Teens are frequently required to read online, and studies show that "college students with higher Internet self-efficacy used computers more correctly and efficiently, solved problems independently rather than asking for help, and were more apt to criticize and question the information they encountered on the Internet."[22]

How and why are public libraries helpful for our teens? A recent study determined that "a majority of fourth graders in the United States are still not reading proficiently, according to a 'Kids Count' report from the Annie E. Casey Foundation. The data show that 80 percent of lower-income

19. Karyn Peterson, "Engaging with Ebooks Can Aid Children's Literacy, Study Finds," *Digital Shift* http://www.thedigitalshift.com/2014/01/k-12/engaging-ebooks-can-aid-childrens-literacy-study-finds/.
20. Peterson, "Engaging with Ebooks."
21. Zickuhr et al., "Young Americans' Library Habits."
22. Julie Coiro, "Understanding Dispositions toward Reading on the Internet," *Journal of Adolescent and Adult Literacy* 55, no. 7 (April 2012).

fourth graders and 66 percent of all kids are not reading at grade level at the start of fourth grade."[23] Libraries can create a nurturing academic environment to give students positive reading experiences and support learning beyond the classroom. The ability to inspire lifelong learners in the library is an important guidepost of libraries and can help teens become effective communicators, engaged citizens, and productive workers. Libraries can assist young people with "skills and attitudes that will prepare them to be responsible, effective, and productive communicators in a free society."[24]

ANECDOTES

- Librarian Kate Aaronson says, "I feel it is very important to get teens into the library and involved so that they grow up knowing the value of having a library available to them and their future kids. I'm finding that many in our communities, especially in the more impoverished areas, do not realize how many free programs and services that the library provides on a daily basis. So the more we can involve teens in volunteering and programs, the better it will be for their present lives and their futures. Moreover their involvement helps the library, so it is a mutually beneficial relationship."
- Librarian Ellen Seeburger, of Braintree's Thayer Public Library, "has tried to increase teen-oriented art and culture programs. Among her successes have been a weeklong creative writing class, a drawing club, and workshops for stop-animation, beading, and constructing miniature hamburgers out of candy. 'Kids come to programs, and they end up staying afterward and looking at materials,' Seeburger says. 'They want to be creative without too much direction.'"[25]

---

23. Karyn Peterson, "US Students Still Struggle with Reading Proficiency, Report Shows," *School Library Journal*, January 28, 2014, http://www.slj.com/2014/01/research/us-students-still-struggle-with-reading-proficiency-report-shows/.
24. Barbara Stripling, "Minors and Internet Interactivity: A New Interpretation of the LBOR," *Knowledge Quest*, September 2010.
25. Williamson, "New Breed of Teen Services Librarians Emerges."

ADDITIONAL RESOURCES

- IMLS. "From Third Place to Makerspace: Public Libraries and Teens." June 2014. Institute of Museum and Library Services. http://www.imls.gov/assets/1/AssetManager/Teens.pdf.
- YALSA. "Teens Need Libraries." American Library Association.
- http://www.ala.org/yalsa/sites/ala.org.yalsa/files/content/professionaltools/Handouts/districtdays_web.pdf.
- YALSA. "What Public Libraries Do for Teens." 2014. American Library Association. http://www.ala.org/yalsa/sites/ala.org.yalsa/files/content/Infographic2_FINAL.pdf.
- YALSA. *YALSA Advocacy Toolkit*. June 2013. American Library Association. http://www.ala.org/yalsa/sites/ala.org.yalsa/files/content/Advocacy%20Toolkit.pdf.

WORKS CITED

ALA, *State of America's Libraries Report 2013 Public Libraries*. 2014. http://www.ala.org/news/state-americas-libraries-report-2013/public-libraries.

ALA, ed. "Teens 13–18 Quick Facts and Statistics." *American Library Association Advocacy*, 2014. http://www.ala.org/advocacy/advleg/advocacyuniversity/additup/13to18/quick.

Braun, Linda W., Maureen L. Hartman, Sandra Hughes-Hassell, and Kafi Kumasi, with contributions from Beth Yoke, *The Future of Library Services for and with Teens: A Call to Action*, January 8, 2014, http://www.ala.org/yaforum/sites/ala.org.yaforum/files/content/YALSA_nationalforum_final.pdf.

Coiro, Julie. "Understanding Dispositions toward Reading on the Internet." *Journal of Adolescent and Adult Literacy* 55, no. 7 (April 2012).

Gaiman, Neil. "Why Our Future Depends on Libraries, Reading and Daydreaming." *Guardian*, October 15, 2013. http://www.theguardian.com/books/2013/oct/15/neil-gaiman-future-libraries-reading-daydreaming.

Harris Interactive, "American Library Association Youth and Library Use Study," June 2007, http://www.ala.org/yalsa/sites/ala.org.yalsa/files/content/professionaltools/HarrisYouthPoll.pdf.

"J. K. Rowling Quotes." *Good Reads*, http://www.goodreads.com/quotes/223272-when-in-doubt-go-to-the-library.

Krashen, Stephen. "Anything but Reading." *Knowledge Quest* 37, no. 5 (May/June 2009).

New York State Library. "The Importance of Summer Reading." NYSED.gov, April 24, 2013. http://www.nysl.nysed.gov/libdev/summer/research.htm.

Peterson, Karyn. "Engaging with Ebooks Can Aid Children's Literacy, Study Finds." *Digital Shift*. http://www.thedigitalshift.com/2014/01/k-12/engaging-ebooks-can-aid-childrens-literacy-study-finds/.

Peterson, Karyn. "US Students Still Struggle with Reading Proficiency, Report Shows." *School Library Journal*, January 28, 2014. http://www.slj.com/2014/01/research/us-students-still-struggle-with-reading-proficiency-report-shows/.

Randall, Rachel. "All Wired Up: Understanding the Reading and Information Searching Behaviors of Teenagers." *YALS* (Summer 2013): 19–22.

Stripling, Barbara. "Minors and Internet Interactivity: A New Interpretation of the LBOR." *Knowledge Quest*, September 2010.

Williamson, Eugenia. "New Breed of Teen Services Librarians Emerges." *Boston Globe*. October 11, 2013. http://www.bostonglobe.com/lifestyle/2013/10/11/new-breed-teen-services-librarians-emerges/mybVRaDDY2mPgezrxMWSmN/story.html.

Zickuhr, Kathryn, et al. "Young Americans' Library Habits and Expectations." *Pew Internet*, June 25, 2013. http://libraries.pewinternet.org/2013/06/25/younger-americans-library-services/.

2

Successfully Managing Teen Behavior for the Benefit of All

TEENAGERS DO NOT always think or behave like adults, and for a good reason: teenagers are undergoing massive developmental changes, both physically and neurologically. This chapter will discuss the effect that the changing teenage brain can have on teen behavior, and how a library worker can take this fact into account when interacting with teen patrons to ensure a positive library experience for both the teen and the library worker. This chapter includes the following:

- A quick guide to teen brain development.
- Step-by-step techniques for managing challenging behavior.

A QUICK GUIDE TO TEEN BRAIN DEVELOPMENT

Imagine a moment in your life when everything is new, your friends and their opinions are the most important part of your existence, and your neurological functioning is undergoing a major rewiring that changes how your brain works—all unbeknownst to you. These are the behind-the-scenes moments of a teenager's development. Studies have shown that "our brains undergo a massive reorganization between our 12th and 25th years."[1] These reorganizations cause teens to behave somewhat unpredictably or in a manner that is confusing to adults, but this behavior is the result of the massive changes that are taking place in teen brains.

---

1. David Dobbs, "Beautiful Brains," *National Geographic*. 220, no. 4 (October 2011): 36.

By providing resources and age-appropriate programs designed with the teenage brain in mind, library staff can help ensure that the library experience is a positive one for everyone.

Teenagers' brains undergo significant changes that impact their current behavior. The frontal cortex—the area of the brain responsible for controlling key functions such as planning, working memory, organization, and mood—experience a growth surge during the teenage years. In a study at the National Institute of Mental Health in Bethesda, Maryland, researchers found that while most of the brain physical structure is in place for a child by the time they are five or six, the prefrontal cortex in teenagers grows again before puberty.[2]

Brain tissues develop by first overproducing and then pruning back the synapses. What Dr. Jay Giedd discovered was that this growth-then-pruning cycle of the synapses occurs again right before puberty (age 11 in girls, 12 in boys), and then there is a pruning and organization during adolescence.[3] Sarah Spinks reports, "Giedd hypothesizes that the growth in gray matter followed by the pruning of connections is a particularly important stage of brain development in which what teens do or do not do can affect them for the rest of their lives. He calls this the 'use it or lose it principle,' and said, 'If a teen is doing music or sports or academics, those are the cells and connections that will be hardwired. If they're lying on the couch or playing video games or MTV, those are the cells and connections that are going to survive.'"[4] This presents an opportunity for library staff to use their talents to provide programming that will not only appeal to their teen patrons but will feed a teen's brain development. Whether attending a makerspace night or a video game club, teens will seek out a library that allows them to find an activity based on their interests and affinities. Library staff who can connect teens with resources, services, and adult mentors that can help them explore their interests are meeting a critical need of teens.

2. Emily Underwood, "Live Chat: The Teen Brain, Jay Giedd, M.D.," *Science*, September 24, 2013, http://news.sciencemag.org/brain-behavior/2013/09/live-chat-teen-brain.
3. Sarah Spinks, "Adolescent Brains Are a Work in Progress: Here's Why," *Frontline*, 2002. http://www.pbs.org/wgbh/pages/frontline/shows/teenbrain/work/adolescent.html.
4. Spinks, "Adolescent Brains."

While the stereotype of an emotional teen has been around for ages, recent studies suggest that there is a scientific reason for this behavior. Deborah Todd, researcher at McLean Hospital in Belmont, Massachusetts, used fMRI scans of teenagers' brains to analyze their reactions to perceive emotions compared to adult brains. She discovered that teenagers' brains evaluate emotional reactions out of a different location in the brain than adults viewing the same images. This could account for the miscommunications, as Todd explains, since "teens mostly used the amygdala, a small almond shaped region that guides instinctual or 'gut' reactions, while the adults relied on the frontal cortex, which governs reason and planning."[5] Thus, teenagers' over-the-top behavior is frequently a result of information in the amygdala part of the brain and the response being processed by the underdeveloped brain. Perhaps this accounts for some of the miscommunication between adults and teenagers. At San Diego State University, volunteers were asked to look at images of people's faces and identify their emotional state. The study determined that teens ages 11–18 had difficulty identifying the emotions. The ability to identify emotions in other humans utilizes the brain's prefrontal cortex.[6] Scientists determined that there is increased nerve activity in the prefrontal cortex during adolescence, which could therefore interfere with interpreting emotions in others.

A QUICK OUTLINE OF THE PARTS OF A TEEN'S BRAIN

- The *amygdala* is the emotional response center of the brain. The *corpus callosum* is the part of the brain that connects right and left hemispheres and is involved with creativity and problem solving. The *frontal cortex* is associated with being the "CEO" of the brain by organizing and strategizing. The *cerebellum* is responsible for coordinating muscle movements and also thinking processes.
- Teens need to be challenged and intrigued by the activities at the library in order for these activities to have a positive influence on

---

5. Deborah Yurgulen-Todd, "Inside the Teenage Brain." *Frontline*, 2014, http://www.pbs.org/wgbh/pages/frontline/shows/teenbrain/interviews/todd.html.

6. "Brain Strain Brings Teen Turmoil," *Current Science* 88, no. 10 (January 3, 2003): 13.

their brain development. Programming that encourages them to collaborate with peers and adult mentors and to be creative will support their developing brain functions. For example, hosting a problem-solving Odyssey of the Mind–type of club or movie/book discussion group will tap into teens' creativity and promote their abilities for strategic thinking.

- Neuroscientists think that young brains are more receptive to learning but that by adolescence learning gets more difficult. According to Angela Brant's research study in psychological science, teens with higher IQs had an extended period of learning going into adolescence. "Brant noticed that kids who had higher IQs to begin with seemed to have an extended period in adolescence during which they retained the ability to learn at a rapid pace, just like much younger children."[7] This study suggests that teens could benefit from learning new, challenging activities in the library, such as acquiring foreign languages, using LEGO robotics, or participating in math and science clubs.

- The brain's development during adolescence is based on decisions that lead to dopamine and the "feel good" sensation or decisions that lead to pain. The brain decreases the options available after adolescence, but strengthens the patterns and specialized connections, according to Dr. Jay Giedd of the NIMH. Dr. Giedd views video games and the Internet as tools that capture the teen brain's reward systems and don't let go, especially the sensation seeking and need for stimulation. In comparison to other biological functions in the brain, reading is a recent activity, "only about 5,200 years old," according to Dr. Giedd.[8] The brain is built to learn by example from watching and observing surrounding people. Dr. Giedd believes that teens will benefit from positive role models in their lives. Library staff can serve as connectors between teens and adult mentors and coaches by reaching out to community members who share an interest with a particular teen patron and

---

7. Shankar Vedantam, "Smart Teenage Brains May Get Some Extra Learning Time," *NPR*, September 23, 2013, http://www.npr.org/blogs/health/2013/09/23/224387862/smart-teenage-brains-may-get-some-extra-learning-time.
8. Underwood, "Live Chat."

by creating opportunities at the library for the adult mentors and coaches to interact with teens.

MANAGING TEENS' BEHAVIOR

Written policies can help ensure that all library patrons know how to behave and what is expected of them in a library setting. They also give library staff leverage when interacting with patrons, because staff can point to the policy as the reason for checking behavior instead of the less productive and more problematic "because I said so" approach. Libraries can become more teen-friendly by taking a positive approach to teen behavior and by creating policies that are fair and consistent across all age groups. Library staff can work with teen patrons to create a list of appropriate behaviors and post it in the library. However, instead of a "Do Not" list, make it a "You Can" list. For example, "You can use the Internet on these computers for 30 minutes and then allow another user their turn." Having a formal Teen Advisory Group (TAG) that gathers teen feedback informally can help you brainstorm ideas for teen-friendly policies for your library space. When enforcing policies with library patrons, it is critical that it is done consistently and uniformly for all patrons across all age groups. Teens are particularly sensitive to issues of fairness.

The "YALSA Teen Services Evaluation Tool" is a helpful guideline for benchmarks in creating a teen-friendly library. The library should "support a culture where all staff act as role models to young adults . . . interacting in a caring, encouraging manner with young adults, modeling responsible behavior and providing clear rules and consequences."[9]

TECHNIQUES FOR MANAGING CHALLENGING BEHAVIOR

Another approach to managing teen behavior requires librarians and library workers to consider that teenagers have a need for control and want to feel heard and respected by their peers and the adults in their

---

9. YALSA, "YALSA Teen Services Evaluation Tool," January 8, 2011, http://www.ala.org/yalsa/sites/ala.org.yalsa/files/content/guidelines/yacompetencies/evaluationtool.pdf.

lives. The psychological suggestions of Jim Fay and Dr. Foster W. Cline are that adults must "lock in our empathy, love, and understanding" in order to manage teens and help them realize that the consequences of their actions directly affect their lives.[10] According to the "Love and Logic" techniques, the adult is not the "bad guy"; instead, the teenager's bad decision becomes the "bad guy" that causes a negative result. This philosophy gives adults and parents a supportive role while the teenager is expected to be respectful and responsible. In a library, this requires adults to remember that some teenagers may need clear expectations for their behavior. If they fail to uphold the library "Do" list of what is acceptable, positive behavior, then librarians and staff must be consistent and yet compassionate with the consequences.

For example, if teen or other patrons are failing to comply with time limits on the computers in the library, a gentle reminder sign posted on each computer is a proactive approach. If a patron continues to ignore the rules, then a conversation with them about the policy is needed. It's important that the conversation focus on the behavior, not the individual. To wind down the conversation, library staff can ask, "What do you think would be a fair consequence for someone who doesn't follow the rules?" Allow teens to develop the consequences for breaking the rules, and then librarians and staff can continue to uphold the rules. Teenagers will respect a library worker's fair and consistent policy enforcement over one who inconsistently enforces policy, is too lenient, or makes exceptions for certain patrons. The idea of "Love and Logic" is to put the idea in the minds of teens and make them realize that their bad decisions cause the consequences, not an adult being "unfair" or "mean to me." Another example of a "Love and Logic" response is as follows with the ineffective technique first and the "Love and Logic" response second:[11]

---

10. Jim Fay and Foster W. Cline, M.D., "What Is Parenting with Love and Logic?," *Love and Logic*, 2013, http://www.loveandlogic.com/t-what-is-for-parents.aspx.
11. Jim Fay, "Turn Your Words into Gold," *Love and Logic*, 1990, http://www.loveandlogic.com/t-Turn-Your-Words-into-Gold.aspx.

Ineffective Response	Love and Logic Response
Please be quiet. It's time to begin.	I'll be glad to start as soon as you show me that you are ready by being seated and sitting quietly.
Stop arguing with me.	I'll be glad to discuss this with you as soon as the arguing stops.

According to the *Love and Logic* website, saying "I'll be glad to discuss this with you as soon as the arguing stops" suggests to teens that the appropriate behavior is their choice. Jim Fay proposes that the problem is the teen's poor choice of arguing and puts the power back in the adult's realm by showing teenagers that their actions are a direct result of their own bad choices.

Emotions run high with teens, and in some cases they might begin yelling or challenging your requests for better behavior. When encountering a challenging emotional outburst situation with a teen, make sure no one is in immediate danger. The upset and angry teen is looking for an outlet, for someone to hear their story. A good listening technique from "Love and Logic" is to say, "I know that you are experiencing a lot of change, but you are capable of keeping your body, your language, and your emotions in control. I believe in you. You can be a good example." This reminds the teen that they can be a better person. Then you can invite them to have a conversation with you instead of yelling and continuing their emotional outburst. You might say, "I can understand how you would feel upset." Acknowledge their feelings and then attempt to get them to talk with you about why they are upset and what they need/want. It doesn't mean you are going to solve the problem immediately, but the conversation may help the teen calm down and feel heard. If the teen will stop arguing, then the librarian or library worker is simply waiting for the good behavior to occur before engaging in discussion with the teenager. While keeping a calm demeanor can be challenging, teenagers will be drawn to library staff who genuinely care about them and about creating a welcoming library for them.

The authenticity of your interest and your ability to personalize the library will help cultivate a welcoming environment for teenagers. At the same time, find occasions to put teens in charge of things that leverage their interests and expertise. For example, if a teen is artistic, ask them to create a display or bulletin board. If a teen is a tech guru, seek their advice in improving the library's social media presence. Their involvement will not only give them a sense of ownership in the library; it also shows them that you value and appreciate them and that they have something of value to offer to the library.

Teenagers define their existence in terms of their interactions with their peers and developing their affinities and passions. As David Dobbs states about adolescents and their developmental traits: "Excitement, novelty, risk, the company of peers. . . . Look deeper, however, and you see that these traits that define adolescence make us more adaptive, both as individuals and as a species. That's doubtless why these traits, broadly defined, seem to show themselves in virtually all human cultures, modern or prehistoric. They may concentrate and express themselves more starkly in modern Western cultures, in which teens spend so much time with each other. But anthropologists have found that virtually all the world's cultures recognize adolescence as a distinct period in which adolescents prefer novelty, excitement, and peers."[12] The teen-friendly library can attract teenagers when it is designed with their developmental needs in mind and when library staff can approach teen patrons with understanding and compassion.

IF YOU THINK A TEEN IS IN DANGEROUS/ABUSIVE SITUATION

If you or any other library worker or patron is in immediate danger, call 911. If a teen confides in you about an abusive situation or if you suspect they are being abused, you must report it. According to the American Humane Association, most states require any professional who works with children to report suspected child abuse or neglect as a "mandated reporter" or as a concerned citizen. "To report suspected

---

12. Dobbs, "Beautiful Brains."

abuse or neglect, contact your local child welfare agency. Depending on your state, this agency may be called the Department of Social Services, Children and Family Services or Human Welfare. The contact number can be found online at http://www.childwelfare.gov/. If you feel that a child is in an emergency situation, however, call 911 or your local law enforcement agency immediately."[13]

A SAMPLE "DO" BEHAVIOR LIST FOR LIBRARIES

Libraries welcome all patrons, including teens, to use and enjoy the facilities, collections, and programs. A teen-friendly library provides a safe environment for all teens of the community to select materials and participate in library programs. These sample rules can apply to all patrons:

- Do ask for recommendations and advice from librarians and library workers.
- Do behave politely and responsibly when using technology equipment.
- Do read quietly without disturbing other people.
- Do enjoy the computers but respect the time limits so that others can also use them.
- Do keep your cell phones on silent so we can all enjoy this space.
- Do save your food/drinks for enjoying outside the library.
- Do remember to check out materials at the front desk.

ADDITIONAL RESOURCES

- YALSA's "Understanding Teen Behavior for a Positive Library Experience" (Chicago: YALSA, 2013): This is a set of training materials that includes eight one-hour modules, a script, handouts, and an annotated bibliography of resources. Learn more at http://www.ala.org/yalsa/young-adults-deserve-best.

---

13. American Humane Association, "Reporting Child Abuse and Neglect," http://www.americanhumane.org/children/stop-child-abuse/fact-sheets/reporting-child-abuse-and-neglect.html.

- YALSA archived webinars (accessible at www.ala.org/yalsa/webinars):
  - "Low-Stress Strategies for Engaging the After-School Crowd" (2013)
  - "Managing the Swarm: Teen Behavior in Libraries and Strategies for Success" (2012)

WORKS CITED

American Humane Association. "Reporting Child Abuse and Neglect." http://www.americanhumane.org/children/stop-child-abuse/fact-sheets/reporting-child-abuse-and-neglect.html.

"Brain Strain Brings Teen Turmoil." *Current Science* 88, no. 10 (January 3, 2003): 13.

Dobbs, David. "Beautiful Brains." *National Geographic* 220, no. 4 (October 2011): 36–59.

Fay, Jim. "Turn Your Words into Gold." *Love and Logic.* 1990. http://www.loveandlogic.com/t-Turn-Your-Words-into-Gold.aspx.

Fay, Jim, and Foster W. Cline, M.D. "What Is Parenting with Love and Logic?" *Love and Logic,* 2013. http://www.loveandlogic.com/t-what-is-for-parents.aspx.

Spinks, Sarah. "Adolescent Brains Are a Work in Progress: Here's Why." *Frontline.* 2002. http://www.pbs.org/wgbh/pages/frontline/shows/teenbrain/work/adolescent.html.

Underwood, Emily. "Live Chat: The Teen Brain, Jay Giedd, M.D." *Science,* September 24, 2013. http://news.sciencemag.org/brain-behavior/2013/09/live-chat-teen-brain.

Vedantam, Shankar. "Smart Teenage Brains May Get Some Extra Learning Time." *NPR,* September 23, 2013. http://www.npr.org/blogs/health/2013/09/23/224387862/smart-teenage-brains-may-get-some-extra-learning-time.

YALSA. "YALSA Teen Services Evaluation Tool." January 8, 2011. http://www.ala.org/yalsa/sites/ala.org.yalsa/files/content/guidelines/yacompetencies/evaluationtool.pdf.

Yurgulen-Todd, Deborah. "Inside the Teenage Brain." *Frontline.* 2014. http://www.pbs.org/wgbh/pages/frontline/shows/teenbrain/interviews/todd.html.

3 | Developing the Teen Collection

THIS CHAPTER WILL provide resources for developing a basic but solid teen collection, whether growing and revitalizing an existing collection or starting from scratch. The variety of materials available for teens— graphic novels and manga, e-books and apps, nonfiction, periodicals, and more—will be touched on in this chapter, as will collection analysis and trend spotting. The chapter will delve into the following:

- How to spot what's popular among teens in your community.
- The top four resources for collection development.
- A five-step plan for building a teen collection from scratch.

Teens have a need to find information about their culture, education, and personal interests. Libraries should promote literacy and lifelong learning with their teen collections. In a survey of teenagers, these three facets were the most important motivators for reading: "Students valued a sense of purpose for the reading, a physical and temporal space to engage in independent reading, and lots of choice among diverse text types to do so."[1] Developing a dynamic teen collection becomes a vital responsibility in a teen-friendly library because the quality of the collection attracts the patrons through the promotion by the library staff. The library is an essential equalizer in providing access both online and

---

1. Douglas Fisher and Nancy Frey, "Motivating Boys to Read," *Journal of Adolescent and Adult Literacy* 55, no. 7 (April 2012).

in print for patrons of different socioeconomic backgrounds. "A study by the Annie E. Casey Foundation found that third-graders who live in poverty—and remember, that's a fifth of the entire country—and read below grade level are three times as likely to drop out as students whose families have never fallen below the poverty line."[2] The library gives students an opportunity to access resources regardless of their income as it promotes literacy.

HOW TO SPOT WHAT'S POPULAR AMONG TEENS IN YOUR COMMUNITY

The first step is to identify the needs of the teens in the community. Some research to gather includes finding out demographic information about teens, including whether or not a significant portion of the teen population speaks English as a second language. A good research resource is the US Census (http://quickfacts.census.gov/qfd/index.html) or the quick links Factfinder page on the US Census website (http://factfinder2.census.gov/faces/nav/jsf/pages/index.xhtml). The Annie E. Casey Foundation's Kids Count (http://www.aecf.org/work/kids-count/) resources are also valuable. Contacting local schools or social service agencies or accessing data from their websites will help you determine the needs of the community's teen population in terms of required reading lists, dominant languages spoken, percentage of students reading at grade level, and so on. As librarian Gretchen Kolderup, Manager for Young Adult Education and Engagement at the New York Public Library, advises:

> *Use demographic information to make a case for such a collection: How many teens are there in your community, and what percentage of the population are they? How do materials for older children (like middle-grade titles) circulate? Does the library at your local middle school or high school have a fiction collection? Is it popular? Where else can teens in your community borrow books or other materials? If you*

---

2. M. Night Shyamalan, "I Got Schooled," *USAIRWAYS*, December 2013.

can demonstrate to your administration with both statistics and anecdotes that there's a need for a teen collection and that it's likely the collection will be used, they're much more likely to approve of creating one.

In terms of materials for leisure reading—will your library need to provide both the hardware and the software for e-reading? What are the schools providing already that the public library probably won't need to focus on? What are required reading lists from the schools that public libraries will be expected to support? What types of careers are your community's teens most interested in pursuing?

Your circulation numbers in the collection and population demographics from the previously mentioned sources will help determine your community's needs, and this data has valid importance for administrators. When looking at building a collection from scratch, the titles may need to be culled from a wide variety of professional and popular sources.

Another way to learn about the needs of the teens in your community is to ask them directly. This can be achieved via online polls or surveys, in-person discussion groups, school visits, and more. In order to be sure that your library is providing what teens need, it is vital that you hear from them in their own words. Not only will this give you valuable information that you can use to tailor your collection and programs, but it also creates buy-in from the teens who see the library as a place that values their opinion and is striving to help them succeed in school and prepare for college and careers.

THE TOP FOUR RESOURCES FOR COLLECTION DEVELOPMENT

1. In One Word: YALSA

The Young Adult Library Services Association (YALSA) recommends teen literature and media via their six annual book and media awards and their seven lists of recommended reading and listening. This organization has been promoting young adult library services and providing professional development for library staff since 1957 as a part of the American

Library Association (ALA). Information on the award winners and lists of recommended reading can be found on their website (www.ala.org/yalsa/booklists). The Michael L. Printz Award is the highest honor that a young adult title can win from YALSA. All of the titles named in YALSA's lists of recommended reading or awards have been collected into the free Teen Book Finder app, available both for Android and Apple platforms. This can be a helpful tool for collection development.

2. Professional Reviews for Young Adult Materials

Many libraries require a positive professional review in order to include an item in the collection. These publications are a sample of respected professional periodicals that include teen materials in their reviews: *School Library Journal*, *Booklist*, *Publishers Weekly*, *Horn Book*. There are also book reviews in the *New York Times Book Review*, the *New York Review of Books*, and many popular professional magazines such as *Voices of Youth Advocates (VOYA)*.

Teenreads (http://www.teenreads.com/) and the Children's Book Council (http://www.cbcbooks.org/news/) both provide a wide variety of what is hot off the presses and upcoming young adult literature reviews.

3. Popular Culture: Movie, Music, and TV Show Tie-in Titles and Current Publishing Trends

It's probably not going to show up in any official professional journals, but the fact that teens love movies, television shows, and online media is an influence in a young adult library collection. The books that are spin-offs or tie-in titles are going to have a huge draw for teen readers even if it is a short-lived season. Whether adults like it or not, teens have an insatiable passion for popular culture, and they want to read about their favorite movie, television, and music icons. Reluctant readers can be one of the more difficult groups to attract, but lists from YALSA such as "Quick Picks for Reluctant Readers" and "Teens Top Ten" include books that are of high interest and with easier reading levels (http://www.ala.org/yalsa/quick-picks-reluctant-young-adult-readers; www.ala.org/yalsa/teenstopten). Another tool for keeping up with teen literature trends is YALSA's blog *The Hub* (www.yalsa.ala.org/thehub/). New content is posted there almost daily, and the archives are searchable.

4. Community: Teen Advisory Group/School Groups/ School Librarians

Finding the time to create a Teen Advisory Group (TAG) may sound daunting, but the dividends are endless for your library. Even if you only have a small group of four or five members, teenagers can offer suggestions on what to purchase for your collection and ideas about alternate formats such as graphic novels, audiobooks, apps, and e-books that are popular with teens. You can also gather this information informally and in ways that are less demanding on your time, via polls on your library website, a teen focus group, and so on. Also, contacting local schools and asking for an opportunity to visit their English or language arts classes might give teens ideas about what your library can offer. School librarians can also provide lists of required reading for their schools. If a visit is not possible, sending out e-mails to local school librarians and asking them to post flyers about library events is a free and easy way to promote your library activities.

Another thought is to reach out to staff at community organizations such as drama/service clubs at high schools or Boy Scouts/Girl Scouts, Boys and Girls Clubs, the Y, after-school programs, et cetera, and invite them to your library to meet the library staff and learn about what resources are available to them and the youth they serve. For example, there might be community groups that help students who are English-language learners that would appreciate having their meeting in your library. While they are visiting, ask for collection suggestions via note cards or set up a brief online survey and ask them to complete the survey on the computer before they leave the library. Make the event fun and welcoming by providing refreshments and door prizes. Be sure to set aside time so that you can learn from them what their needs are, and talk about ways that you might work together to help improve the lives of teens in your community.

GROWING AND REVITALIZING AN EXISTING COLLECTION

E-books/Audiobooks/Alternative Formats

Using alternative formats—especially materials that are designed with high-interest/low-reading levels—have long been useful tools for library staff in reaching reluctant readers. Audiobooks are an essential part of the collection as many readers prefer listening to an audiobook or benefit from the combination of listening to and reading a book. Struggling readers and readers who are learning English in particular benefit from following along in the printed book while listening to a recording. According to a 2011 interest inventory study, there were "no statistically significant differences in comprehension across print, e-book, and audiobook modalities. Participants' levels of comprehension for each text were the same regardless of the format in which it was received. There was also no difference in engagement across modalities; the amount of interest participants expressed in a text was the same regardless of the format in which it was received."[3] In other words, students were equally engaged in a book regardless of the format.

E-books are the newest iteration of digital media, and utilizing them often depends on the flexibility of your library as well as the needs of your community members. Are e-readers available for circulation? Do patrons have to bring their own devices? Is there a digital lending system in place, or is it cumbersome to download e-books? E-books are important formats to consider; however, first determine the need/demand, and then consider the infrastructure that must be put in place to support these formats. Teens will begin to expect these digital items in libraries as more schools and families provide reading experiences on e-readers, smartphones, and tablets.

Graphic novels and manga are another popular format that should be included in a teen library, and, as with audiobooks, these offer a similar benefit to struggling readers and English-language learners. The images

---

3. Jessica Moyer, "What Does It Really Mean to 'Read' a Text?" *Journal of Adolescent and Adult Literacy* 55, no. 3 (November 2011).

in comics and graphic novels serve as a tool to help an individual interpret the text. YALSA has a list of "Great Graphic Novels for Teens" that will help you start or improve a collection at your library (http://www.ala.org/yalsa/ggnt).

Databases/Websites/Digital Resources

A twenty-first-century library collection is more than books and printed materials. Providing electronic resources for teen patrons can be costly and sometimes time-consuming. Before investing in any databases, it's essential to find out what is already widely available to teens, either through the school system or state library agency, and then making sure it's accessible from your library's website and computers. After conducting this research, identify any gaps in materials and then seek out databases to fill those particular needs. The American Association of School Librarians (AASL) provides a list of recommended websites that is updated annually (www.ala.org/aasl/standards-guidelines/best-websites), and both AASL and YALSA provide recommendations for mobile apps. YALSA does this via its "App of the Week" feature on the YALSAblog (http://yalsa.ala.org/blog/); AASL compiles an annual list of recommended apps (www.ala.org/aasl/standards-guidelines/best-apps).

Your teen patrons can be surveyed to discover what websites and other media they use for school assignments and to pursue leisure activities. A teen volunteer could be tapped to create and periodically update a list of these resources for the library's website.

Local Information, History, Et Cetera

Some of us may remember the "vertical files" that were common in libraries before the advent of the Internet. These were collections of pamphlets, photos, brochures, maps, and so on that often focused on local events, points of interest, and other topics. There is still a need for patrons to have access to local information. The library can decide the best strategy for collecting and maintaining this resource, whether it's print, digital, or a combination of both. Teen patrons can be asked to contribute, for example, by collecting photos or creating a documentary about some aspect of local history. People in the community are another vital part of a local collection. Teens need access to trusted adult experts, coaches, and mentors in order to expand their knowledge and pursue interest-based learning. Libraries can compile lists of community experts and keep those on hand for instances when a teen is looking for someone to help them learn more about graphic design, filmmaking, or whatever their interest is. Some libraries hold "Living Book" events where community members are brought in to talk about a particular subject, life experience, or historical event that they witnessed.

Special Collections

Today's libraries are thinking "outside of the book" and providing special collections based on community needs and interests. For example, libraries are lending kitchen gadgets, gardening and construction tools, craft equipment like sewing machines, and more based on what the community demand is. Often times these special collections consist of items that are too costly for many community members to invest in or items that are not used often enough to justify purchasing the item. For example, a library could have an extensive cake pan collection that it lends out to patrons, who otherwise would have to incur the expense of buying a cake pan for a single use (for example, their son wants a birthday party with a particular theme and the parent wants to bake a cake to go with the theme). Teens in particular do not have much spending money for expensive items like prom gowns and tuxedos, so finding out what their needs are and working with a community partner to create a lending library designed to fill that need can be an enormous help to teens and be yet another way that your library demonstrates its value to the community.

HOW TO START A YOUNG ADULT LIBRARY COLLECTION:
An Interview with Librarian Gretchen Kolderup

Librarian Gretchen Kolderup, Manager for Young Adult Education and Engagement at the New York Public Library, shared her insights to improve your YA collection.

1. **What types of materials should be included in a young adult library collection (that's being created from scratch)?**

   It really depends on the community. I think that's one of the most important tenets of collection development: What's popular in one library won't be in another, and you need to know your patrons and their tastes to develop a collection that will meet their needs. That said, current fiction aimed at teens is a great place to begin if you're starting from scratch. If you have the space and money for more, buy graphic novels, award-winning fiction, classics, or other required reading that will be used for school assignments, and high-interest nonfiction. If you still have money and space, go for magazines that will appeal to teens. And depending on the needs and interests of your teens, you may also find hi-lo titles [high-interest, low-reading level], audiobooks and Playaways, and titles written in languages other than English to be useful. If your library has the budget and the technological capabilities, be sure to include e-books and apps.

2. **What specific collection development resources would you consult for recommendations?**

   Your teens should be your top resource. What are they interested in? What are they reading? What are their friends reading? How do they find out about great new books? Talk to parents and teachers, also, to get a sense for what your community's interests and needs are. Beyond people resources, the *New York Times* Best Seller lists are a good place to start for popular current fiction (they have lists for YA books, middle-grade books, and YA/children's series).

   For a more comprehensive resource, turn to the Young Adult Library Services Association (YALSA). Every year, librarians across the country work together to select novels, nonfiction, graphic novels, and more to win awards and be recognized on lists of the best YA materials from the previous year. The awards are announced at the Youth Media Awards (YMAs) in January, and the lists are published shortly afterward. The lists are especially helpful because they include titles that aren't just from the previous year (the "Popular Paperbacks" list), books that will appeal to reluctant readers (the "Quick Picks" list), and books in other formats (like the "Amazing Audiobooks" list). YALSA's "Teens' Top Ten" is announced at a different time, but the books on the list are chosen by actual teens nationwide, so it's a good barometer for popular titles.

Once your collection is more established and you're looking for ongoing resources to use, check out professional review sources like *VOYA*, *School Library Journal* (not just for school librarians!), *Kirkus Reviews*, and *Publishers Weekly*. Professionals in the publishing and library world evaluate books on their literary quality and appeal to teens, which will help you discover new books and decide if a particular title is right for your library. *VOYA* is particularly helpful since each book is rated both on quality and popularity, which will help you build your collection. Some sources even review apps and enhanced e-books.

There's also a large, active book blogging community online, and a lot of readers and reviewers of YA books on Goodreads.com. YALSA also hosts a few e-mail Listservs where librarians, English teachers, and others who love YA lit talk about current titles, read-alikes, and more. The more you can immerse yourself in the world of YA literature, the better you'll know the books.

3. **How should library professionals/librarians research what's popular in their community (pop culture/trends/ minorities in community, etc.)?**

Your community members themselves are the best place to start! If there are already teens hanging out at your library, start by observing them: What do they do while they're there? Are they playing games or watching videos? Reading? Strike up conversations about what they're doing; if you're genuinely interested, they'll respond positively to that.

If talking to teens isn't possible yet, talk to parents and teachers (or other librarians—like the one at the public library if you're in a school, or the one at the school if you're in a public library) to find out what your teens' interests are and what's going on in their lives. You can also see if there are local bloggers whom you can follow to get a sense for what's happening in your community. For more databased information like demographics, the US Census is a great source.

4. **What is the value of researching your library circulation usage? How could you make a case for a YA library without prior statistics (if you were starting a collection, for example)?** Once you have a collection, knowing how well the items you chose are circulating is essential! You'll want to track overall trends (Did more books get checked out in May this year than the year before?), as well as digging into which titles are circulating and which ones aren't. If a title isn't being checked out, you should remove it from the collection and think about why your teens aren't interested in it. Is that genre just not something your teens like? Was the cover unappealing? Is the title older and has its popularity just run its course? Is the book just in physically poor condition and would a replacement be checked out? If your teens consistently check out books about vampires or road trips or skateboarding, use that knowledge when you buy new titles.

If your library doesn't have a YA collection, use demographic information to make a case for such a collection: How many teens are there in your community, and what percentage of the population are they? How do materials for older children (like middle-grade titles) circulate? Does the library at your local middle school or high school have a fiction collection? Is it popular? Where else can teens in your community borrow books? If you can demonstrate to your administration with both statistics and anecdotes that there's a need for a YA collection and that it's likely the collection will be used, they're much more likely to approve of creating one.

And while a YA collection should be developed primarily for teens, a growing number of adults also read YA titles. If your administration is hesitant about creating a YA section, see if you can start purchasing YA titles that will be shelved in the adult section. Adults will discover them and read them, and you can start recommending them to teens as well. Once these books have been circulating for a while, you'll have statistics to help you build your case for a separate YA collection.

5. **How do you include digital items—e-books, video games, and apps—in the YA collection? What other important resources should be included in the collection?**
This really depends on your community, your library, and your technological capabilities. Teens have grown up in a distinctly multimedia world, so including e-books, video games, apps, DVDs, CDs, downloadable music, and other non-print sources in your collection is important. What kinds of multimedia does your library already offer? Can you start offering content that will appeal to teens in those same formats?

Digital content can be difficult to promote; with a physical book, you can put it on display or put it directly into a teen's hands. If your library also offers e-books, how will you make sure teens know you're doing so? Signs in the teen space or promotional spots on the library's website will help, but you may also want to offer to visit classes at schools to actually demonstrate how to download an e-book.

You'll also need to consider whether or not your library will offer devices along with content. If you're making e-books available to your patrons but none of them have e-readers, smartphones, or computers at home, they're not going to be able to take advantage of what you offer. Even if circulating devices is outside the realm of possibility, could teens use these devices within the library?

6. **What is a good strategy to incorporate different reading levels and ESL books (from patrons' languages in your community) in your YA collection?**
It's important to know what your community's needs are as you're planning your collection. If you have a large population of teens for whom English isn't their first language, make sure you have books in the languages they speak and read! Make these books easy to find: shelve them in a prominent area, and have signs in that language directing people to what you have.

Books that are written at a lower reading level (but are still at an interest or content level that teens will find engaging) are a little trickier: teens who need these materials may not be comfortable identifying themselves that way, so you may want to shelve them with the mainstream titles and then have a finding aid (like a booklist or a bookmark) that you can offer to them or to their parents or teachers to help them locate those items. Some publishers have imprints specifically for hi-lo books; you can also consult things like the Lexile level of a book to get a sense for how complex the language in a book is. (But keep in mind that the Lexile level is only a measure of text complexity and doesn't measure how mature the content or how sophisticated the ideas in the book are.)

Alternate formats can also help teens who read at a lower level. Pairing an audiobook with the print title can help teens to hear the pronunciation of words, and they may be more engaged by a narrator who brings emotion to the text—just make sure you choose audiobooks that are performed well! Graphic novels often appeal to teens with lower reading levels because they can use the visual content (like characters' facial features or body language) to better understand the text.

7. **How can you maximize the partnerships between your library with local schools/clubs/community organizations?** In my experience, most of these partnerships are built on relationships between people at those organizations, so start by going to the schools, clubs, and community organizations you'd like to partner with and introducing yourself. Have a clear sense of your library's mission, and ask about what the partner organization's mission and current priorities are. Where their focus and yours overlap is where partnerships should be built—and if there's no common ground, that organization isn't the right one for you to work with.

If you can, come to the organization with a plan: "We know that a lot of students hang out at your youth center after school. Would you be interested in having a collection of paperbacks here that kids could read and borrow? I'd be happy to bring new titles over every month and take out the ones that are less popular." People are more likely to say yes to a partnership if they can work with you on something that's already coming along.

Teens themselves can also be good connections to organizations: if the president of the school's technology club hangs out at your library frequently, talk to her about the club and what they're up to, and then suggest ways for the library and the club to work together. She'll be a natural go-between and can introduce you to other students and the faculty adviser. Similarly, get to know the officers in the school government if you can; they'll keep you updated about activities going on at the school.

Especially if you're just starting out, building partnerships with other organizations is a great way to meet teens in your community and get the word out about the library. It takes work and time to build those relationships, but it's how you'll reach teens who aren't already library users.

ADDITIONAL RESOURCES

- Reads 4 Teens, www.ala.org/yalsa/reads4teens
- YALSA archived webinars (accessible at www.ala.org/yalsa/webinars)
  - "Building Blocks for a Diverse Library Collection" (2013)
  - "Reaching Reluctant Readers" (2012)
  - "Thinking Outside the Book to Serve Your Teen Patrons' Needs" (2014)

WORKS CITED

Fisher, Douglas, and Nancy Frey. "Motivating Boys to Read." *Journal of Adolescent and Adult Literacy* 55, no. 7 (April 2012).

Moyer, Jessica. "What Does It Really Mean to 'Read' a Text?" *Journal of Adolescent and Adult Literacy* 55, no. 3 (November 2011).

Shyamalan, M. Night. "I Got Schooled." *USAIRWAYS*, December 2013.

4 | Making a Welcoming Space for Teens

JUST AS NOT all libraries have the capacity to have a teen services librarian on staff, not all have the ability to have a designated teen space. This chapter will discuss the importance of having a teen-friendly library, how to develop policies governing teen spaces, and resources to consult when developing a teen space. Teen ownership and involvement in planning and managing teen spaces are essential components and will also be explored. This chapter covers the following:

- Resources for designing your teen space.
- Real-life before-and-after examples of teen spaces.
- Sample policies and rules for teen spaces.

Libraries are centers of learning and discovery that create opportunities for teenagers to discover a new book, learn a new skill, or participate in a group activity that encourages creativity and problem solving, such as maker programs or LEGO robotics. Teen spaces can be created in existing libraries by organizing the teen collection and highlighting a section of the library as their area. Teen-friendly libraries can welcome new teen patrons and make regulars happy if there is a space dedicated to them. Teen-friendly libraries help call attention to the opportunities that the library offers to teens and serve as a vehicle that supports their developmental needs. According to Dr. Daniel Siegel in his book *Brainstorm*, teenagers need an outlet for creative expression and engagement. Dr. Siegel posits, "The way the brain is changing really is urging [adolescents] to try new things, to have an emotional spark that pushes them forward, a social engagement with their peers, a search for novelty. . . . So we [adults] want to give them an internal compass to know what has meaning, what's important to them. . . . And my hope for all of us is that if we rethink how to have a cultural conversation around adolescence, seeing the courage and creativity that's there."[1] Libraries provide that safe space for teens to have a social outlet, engage their brain, and seek intellectual challenges.

The Search Institute has identified forty developmental assets that are necessary for healthy development of adolescents. Of these, the "community values youth," "creative activities," and "youth programs" are in the top tier and apply to the teen spaces in public libraries.[2] According to a 2007 study, library use is increasing, with 78% of children ages 8–18 having library cards.[3] And the appeal of free access to books and technology can continue to increase library usage in the future.

One of the key elements of an effective teen space is creating it in partnership and collaboration with teens. In a research study by the University of Washington in 2010, nearly one in three Americans ages 14 or older—roughly 77 million people—used a public library.[4] This illustrates the importance of libraries as collaborative partners in communities around the United States. Besides getting input from teens themselves, your local community's teen clubs, such as Boy Scouts and Girl Scouts, as well as local schools might also provide insights into what teens in your community value in their library spaces.

According to YALSA's "Teen Space Guidelines," the most important factors in a teen library space are the following attributes:

- Solicit teen feedback and input in the design and creation of the teen space.

---

1. Daniel Siegel, M.D., "Teenagers Are 'Crazy' but Expert Says Behavior Is Vital to Development," *NPR*, January 28, 2014, http://www.npr.org/2014/01/28/267608451/teenagers-are-crazy-but-expert-says-behavior-is-vital-to-development.
2. "40 Developmental Assets for Adolescents," *Search Institute*, 2007, http://www.search-institute.org/content/40-developmental-assets-adolescents-ages-12-18.
3. Kimberly Bolan, "The Need for Teen Spaces in Public Libraries," *YALSA*, 2008, http://www.ala.org/yalsa/guidelines/whitepapers/teenspaces.
4. Gates Foundation, "IMLS Research Proves Patrons Value Online Access," *American Libraries Magazine* (May 2010): 19.

- Provide a library environment that encourages the emotional, social, and intellectual development of teens.
- Provide a library space for teens that reflects the community in which they live.
- Provide and promote materials that support the educational and leisure needs of teens.
- Ensure that the teen space has appropriate acceptable use and age policies to make teens feel welcome and safe.
- Provide furniture and technology that is practical yet adaptive.[5]

These YALSA suggestions are based on a wealth of personal experience and professional expertise. According to Professor Anthony Bernier, libraries should follow five basic rules for arranging their seating for teens:

1. Maximize the options at our disposal.
2. Mix and don't match.
3. Offer movement in furniture. (Don't think that everything has to stay in the same place all the time, and think about swiveling furniture and rocking furniture!)
4. Explore the floor with carpeting, funky furniture, and platforms.
5. Libraries should move away from **privileging the collection to privileging the social experience that libraries can support.**[6]

Even if your library cannot create a totally separate space for teens, ask your teen patrons what they would like to have as far as décor, comfortable seating, and so on. Also, think about how you can actively engage teens in creating the space and making it their own. Is one of the teen patrons artistic, and could they create a poster for the library? You could then frame it at a local craft store and hang it near the young adult bookshelves. Creating a sense of individuality for the young adults in

---

5. YALSA, "Teen Space Guidelines," 2011–2012, http://www.ala.org/yalsa/guidelines/teenspaces.
6. Kelly Tyler, "President's Program: The Teen Third Space," *YALSAblog*, July 5, 2008, http://yalsa.ala.org/blog/2008/07/05/presidents-program-the-teen-third-space/.

your community could be as easy as buying some ALA "Read" posters with current movie stars and putting some chairs and tables near the young adult shelves along with some colorful decorations.

LIBRARIAN GRETCHEN KOLDERUP'S IDEAS FOR TEEN SPACES

The design of teen spaces varies from community needs, budget, and facilities in your library. As the Manager for Young Adult Education and Engagement at the New York Public Library, librarian Gretchen Kolderup has some quick-start ideas to improve your teen library space. In her experiences at the New York Public Library, these were important ideas for teen spaces.

1. **What are essential ideas in creating a teen space in the library? Are there important resources to consult in order to create teen-friendly spaces and the rules governing these spaces?**

   The fundamental idea in a teen space is that it be for teens. That is, the space should be exclusively for them (not a space they have to share with children or adults); it should meet their needs (whether that's room to read, to do homework alone or in groups, to hang out, to do library programs—or all of these things); and it should be a space they've helped create.

   As always, teens themselves are the most important part of the equation and your best resource! During the planning process, get their input at every step along the way—or involve them directly in the planning. Work with your teens—through a Teen Advisory Group, for example—to learn about how they use the space, what furniture they think is comfortable, and how they envision the look and layout of the space. Involving teens directly in the planning process for creating the rules for the space is also key: they're much more likely to follow the rules and to remind their friends to do so as well if they helped come up with them. YALSA also created a set of guidelines for teen spaces (http://www.ala.org/yalsa/guidelines/teens-paces) that goes into a lot more detail about every aspect of space planning. This is not just an essential but also a definitive resource.

2. **How does a library professional design programs that highlight the new collection and also create buzz so that teens will attend?**
   This can be difficult if you're just getting started. Use relationships you've built with other organizations or with teens who already visit your library to bring in new teens. Offer to visit classes at the school to talk up new titles or to offer personalized recommendations for students. Make sure that advertisements for your programs get placed where both teens and their parents will notice them.

   If you're really focused on growth, you can promise prizes or privileges to teens who bring a friend to a program. If you have a Teen Advisory Group, use them as your street team and have them distribute flyers at school or other places where they and their friends congregate, and have them talk up the library at other clubs they belong to. Multiple academic studies have found that teens' top information source is their peers, so word of mouth is one of your most powerful tools in getting information out about what your library does.

3. **What types of teen involvement could exist in this new YA library space?**
   If teens see themselves and their interests reflected in the teen space in the library, they'll feel more ownership of the space and they'll be more engaged with what you do. If you don't already have a Teen Advisory Group, start one.

Invite teens to contribute something to the physical space, whether that's having your power readers take over a display shelf and keep it stocked with their favorites, giving your TAG members bookends to paint, or working with the art class at the school to display student art. As you get to know your teens and build relationships with them, use them to help design and run programs, create flyers, or contribute to the teen space in a way that makes use of their interests and skills. Have your teens write reviews and display those reviews with the books. Publish their reviews on Tumblr or Facebook. Have a reward system for teens who help keep the space in order, contribute content for your blog or displays, or advertise your programs outside the library. If your library already has a volunteer program, find out how many of your volunteers are teens. If you already have teen volunteers, see if you can have them spend their time in your teen space. If you don't have teen volunteers, start a teen volunteering program! There may be young people in your community who need service hours for school, church, or legal reasons—why not have them do their hours at the library?

But most importantly, find out what your teens enjoy doing and what they want to contribute, and then give them avenues to do so! One of the best parts of working with teens is that they're developing skills and interests, and the library can help them build on these skills and deepen their interests. You can help them grow as people by giving them opportunities to try new things and to learn more—that's very powerful!

ADA COMPLIANCE FAST FACTS

- Remember to check with your library policies on being ADA (Americans with Disabilities Act) compliant in all spaces.

- In general, all areas of the library—reading, study areas, stacks, and reference should be accessible.
- According to the ALA website, "The minimum required space between the stacks for wheelchair access is 36 inches. The space that is *preferred*—and this word makes the difference—is 42 inches.
- The ALA has guidelines and explanations at their website (http://www.ala.org/tools/ada-and-libraries).
- The ALA factsheet also includes books and web links to library planning guides (http://www.ala.org/tools/libfactsheets/alalibraryfactsheet11).
- The Association of Specialized and Cooperative Library Agencies (ASCLA) provides resources to help libraries ensure that their space is accommodating to people with various physical challenges. Check out their website for resources: www.ala.org/ascla/asclaissues/issues.

CREATING TEEN SPACES ON A SMALL BUDGET

With the myriad of challenges facing libraries today, it's not surprising that the infamous B-word (budget!) comes up when planning a teen space and looking for funds. Here are some helpful hints and ideas for how to find the funding or creative ways to stretch a budget.

- Think about the partnerships that your library already has in place. Could the Friends of the Library group sponsor a couple of chairs or a bookshelf, or provide volunteers to do some painting? You could even ask your library supervisor if anyone in the Friends group has connections with local businesses such as big box stores. Sometimes these businesses have clearance items that could include furniture.
- Reach out to local businesses such as home improvement stores for discounts or donations, such as on paint, shelving, and supplies.
- Ask the local community college library or college library if they have old but gently used furniture they would be willing to donate.
- Local schools may be willing to help you with volunteers from service clubs if you need help moving furniture or stacks of books.

- Contact teachers in the vocational department of your local school to see if they could provide assistance with certain aspects of the project, such as creating a floor plan or building bookshelves.
- Librarian Emily Brown suggests designing a floor plan and using measurements to configure the space before you start spending money. Ms. Brown states, "Tables and chairs (and coffee tables and stools and ottomans) need to be complementary in height, and the space between furniture is as important as the furniture."[7] Mobile apps exist, such as Floorplan Creator and Magic Plan, to help you come up with a quality floor plan.
- You may have to start small and phase things in over a few years as the budget allows.
- For small spaces, invest in a sturdy cart or two so you can put things like printers and other equipment on them and they can be moved as needed, or placed in storage during an event.

The following ideas are the suggestions from librarian April Pavis and the *YALSAblog*.

- *Idea #1:* Ask the folks in Circulation for more shelf space for YA books. With their approval, shift adult books (or whatever is keeping you from expanding) away from the YA collection, giving yourself space to work with. Even if you don't need the shelf space, you can use the more spread-out shelves to hold program flyers, set up book displays, hold bookmarks, display teen artwork, and more. Short on time? Use volunteers! Teen volunteers are probably (hopefully?) the same teens who will be utilizing the Teen Space. Therefore, use them to help you shift. Offer volunteer/service hours or library card fine amnesty in return for their time.
- *Idea #2:* Have a Teen Center that pops up wherever you have space. If you can't have permanent space in your building, plan a weekly pop-up in your library's meeting room or children's storytime room.

---

7. Emily Brown, "Teen Space on a Dime," *YALSAblog*, April 14, 2010, http://yalsa.ala.org/blog/2010/04/14/teen-space-on-a-dime/.

Bring TVs and gaming systems, laptop computers, a cart of new YA books, craft supplies, et cetera. Move the day and time around as it suits the needs of your teens, but try to do this on a regular basis.

- *Idea #3:* Take that pop-up Teen Center to a local community center or school. Load up your car with all of the necessary equipment and set up shop in the non-library space. Plan this alongside a school's after-school tutoring program (maybe to begin immediately after tutoring sessions), and watch your attendance skyrocket. While teens play games, tell them about the library and invite them to visit and say hello to you next time they visit. *Have a special treat to give to the teens who do visit the library and seek you out. If possible, give them a teen-friendly tour of the branch and maybe even introduce them to a couple coworkers. Prove to them that they are welcome.

- *Idea #4:* You know all those computers and comfy chairs in the adult area? Teens like those, too. Move a couple of each closer to the teen shelves. This encourages teens to be comfortable in their own space, even if it's a mere 20 feet from the adult area. Put a sign over the computers and chairs informing customers that they are for teens only (during non-school hours). *This will likely result in angry adult users once in a while. The "my tax dollars" fight will begin, but if you and the entire staff stand your ground, this won't continue forever.

- *Idea #5:* If you have a bit of spare money (Or receive a grant? Or win the lottery? Or acquire a millionaire benefactor?), purchase teen-friendly furniture and computers (Macs?) instead of just taking away from the adult area (à la idea #4). Put a plaque on the wall near all of this new stuff describing the area as a teen space and thanking those who supported it (the board, director, etc.). That way teens and adults who scope out the area know who it is for and why it is there. *Using private funds such as a donation or grant for these items will allow you to say, "These were not purchased with tax dollars," which is a great way to put the kibosh on the ol' "my tax dollars!" argument.

- *Idea #6:* Display YA books and program flyers in the places where teens are (i.e., computer banks, study carrels, etc.). Maybe your teen patrons don't know you own entire shelves of YA books, magazines, and audiobooks. A sign pointing them in the right direction will not only inform them—it will inform your community that your library cares for teens and wants to provide services specifically for them. Be creative with your displays (tape arrows to the floor to literally guide them to the materials).

- *Idea #7:* Even if you cannot shift books, set up a teen-only computer station or buy comfy furniture to put near the teen stacks to make the teen stacks stand out. Cover the shelving units in bright-colored paper. Have teens make posters to tape to the shelves or hang from the ceiling over the shelves. The possibilities go on and on. Paint the walls nearest to the stacks, even! Delineate the Teen Center from the rest of the library. Whatever you choose to do, try to do it with a few teen volunteers. Making them a part of the library gives what you do that much more meaning.[8]

VIRTUAL TEEN SPACES

Angela Sigg, from the Denver Public Library, suggests that "since teens don't remember life before the Internet, it is only appropriate to think of a library's website as an extension of the library's physical space." Sigg offers several ideas for making your website a teen's virtual third library space:

- Brainstorm with teens—the space is for them, so ask them what they want.
- Get feedback from staff.
- Consider setting up a wiki to show mock-ups of the site.
- Look at other teen library websites for inspiration.
- Think about ways to bring teens back with fresh content. Denver Public Library has integrated podcasting and podcasting workshops, YouTube contests, original teen art, and teen reviews (their most popular feature).

---

8. April Pavis, "How to Create a Teen Space Out of Nothing," *YALSAblog*, September 30, 2011, http://yalsa.ala.org/blog/2011/09/30/how-to-create-a-teen-space-out-of-nothing.

Sigg warns that there are several pitfalls to avoid in building your website as well. So if you want to do one, keep these in mind:

- Too much text. Teens don't want their third space to feel too much like being in school.
- Being boring. It's the kiss of death.
- Trying to talk like teens. It just won't work.
- Not continually offering new content. Commit to keeping it fresh so teens have a reason to return often.
- Not listening to what teens think. It's their site, they should like it![9]

When designing your website for teens, consult YALSA's "Teen Space Guidelines," because that document includes information about virtual spaces.

WHEN THERE'S ABSOLUTELY NO ROOM FOR A DEDICATED TEEN SPACE

Tiny libraries just don't have the luxury of having unique spaces for different patron groups. When that's the case, it's important to look at the library as a whole and determine whether it is welcoming to teens and accommodating to their unique needs. Strategies for making a library appealing to and accommodating of teens include the following:

- Use color for the walls, furniture, carpeting, etc.
- Display posters and other visuals of contemporary individuals that appeal to teens, such as those of YA authors, actors, musicians, etc.
- Incorporate teen art into the décor, whether it's something more permanent, like a mural, or just a temporary art exhibition of teen work (a great opportunity to partner with the art teacher at the local school).
- Ensure there's adequate signage so things can be found easily. Teen patrons, especially, can be reluctant to ask for help and can benefit from visual cues.

---

9. Tyler, "President's Program: The Teen Third Space."

- Use inclusive language on signage, brochures, and so on, by making sure to use the word "teens." Teens don't want to be referred to as "children."
- Rotate displays of books and other materials of interest to teens.
- Avoid lumping teen materials and items in with children's, as teens will shy away from anything that they feel is too juvenile.
- Have a flexible space—chairs, tables, carts, even bookshelves that are on wheels or that are mobile can help you transform the library space as needed for events for specific audiences.
- Provide a range of seating options. Teens sit in hard, upright chairs all day at school. Libraries can provide armchairs, floor cushions, bean bag chairs, and more. Additionally, teens have a developmental need to be social, so strive to create a seating option where a small group of teens can gather and talk without disturbing other patrons.
- Consider a road trip—hold programs and events outside of the library at places in the community where teens gather.
- Leverage outdoor space so that in good weather teens can study or read a book outside the library on benches and other outdoor furniture (perhaps there's a local landscape company that could volunteer time in creating a welcoming outdoor space).

ADDITIONAL RESOURCES

- YALSA archived webinars (accessible at www.ala.org/yalsa/webinars):
  - "Best Practices in Teen Space Design" (2011)
  - "Check In: Makerspaces 101, Teens and You" (2013)
  - "Teen Spaces on a Dime" (2012)
  - "Welcoming Spaces: Serving Patrons with ASD (Autism Spectrum Disorder)" (2014)
- YALSA makerspace resources wiki page: http://wikis.ala.org/yalsa/index.php/Maker_%26_DIY_Programs.

WORKS CITED

ALA. "ADA and Libraries." 1996–2014. http://www.ala.org/tools/ada-and-libraries.

Bolan, Kimberly. "The Need for Teen Spaces in Public Libraries." *YALSA*. 2008. http://www.ala.org/yalsa/guidelines/whitepapers/teenspaces.

Brown, Emily. "Teen Space on a Dime." *YALSAblog*. April 14, 2014. http://yalsa.ala.org/blog/2010/04/14/teen-space-on-a-dime/.

"40 Developmental Assets for Adolescents," *Search Institute*, 2007, http://www.search-institute.org/content/40-developmental-assets-adolescents-ages-12-18.

Gates Foundation. "IMLS Research Proves Patrons Value Online Access." *American Libraries Magazine* (May 2010): 19.

Pavis, April. "How to Create a Teen Space Out of Nothing." *YALSAblog*. September 30, 2011. http://yalsa.ala.org/blog/2011/09/30/how-to-create-a-teen-space-out-of-nothing/.

Siegel, Daniel, M.D. "Teenagers Are 'Crazy' but Expert Says Behavior Is Vital to Development." *NPR*. January 28, 2014. http://www.npr.org/2014/01/28/267608451/teenagers-are-crazy-but-expert-says-behavior-is-vital-to-development.

Tyler, Kelly. "President's Program: The Teen Third Space." *YALSAblog*. July 5, 2008. http://yalsa.ala.org/blog/2008/07/05/presidents-program-the-teen-third-space/.

YALSA, "Teen Space Guidelines." 2011–2012. http://www.ala.org/yalsa/guidelines/teenspaces.

5 | Programming

HOSTING PROGRAMS AND events for and with teens is an important service that a library provides to its community. Library programs provide teens with a safe, neutral place to meet other teens, socialize, and learn new things—helping them channel their energy into positive activities that can prepare them for college and careers. This chapter will cover resources for program inspiration and ideas for inexpensive and easy-to-run programs, as well as methods to market and promote teen library programs, including the following:

- *Programs-in-a-Box:* plans and supply lists for popular, simple programs.
- *Planning a Teen Summer Reading/Learning Program:* the bare bones list, including ideas for activities, incentives, marketing, and design.

According to the YALSA report *The Future of Library Services for and with Teens*, Libraries need to embrace "our role as facilitator rather than expert" and refocus "beyond our traditional roles and measurements of success" by partnering with community organizations to teach job skills for teens.[1] Teens from low-income families in particular benefit from library programming, as they may not be able to afford things like

---

1.–Linda W. Braun, Maureen L. Hartman, Sandra Hughes-Hassell, and Kafi Kumasi, with contributions from Beth Yoke, *The Future of Library Services for and with Teens: A Call to Action*, January 8, 2014, http://www.ala.org/yaforum/sites/ala.org.yaforum/files/content/YALSA_nationalforum_final.pdf.

art and music classes, memberships at the Y, the fees and dues needed to participate in extracurricular activities, or the cost of the latest tech gadgets and digital tools they need to learn how to use to prepare for twenty-first-century jobs.

Consistent, high-quality teen programming also helps libraries create a positive and lasting relationship with teens in the community. Corporations know how important it is to target young people through advertising and marketing because brand loyalty, once established, can last a lifetime. The library can generate its own kind of "brand loyalty" by creating many positive experiences for teen patrons to participate in. The teens of today are the voters, decision makers, and leaders of the future, and if they remember doing interesting, exciting things at the library, how much more likely are they to grow up to value and support libraries?

Libraries can fill a real community need by helping teens with college and career preparation—especially underserved populations of teens. YALSA-authored *The Future of Libraries for and with Teens: A Call to Action* highlights the pivotal role of libraries for teens at this juncture between school and careers. The report states that there is a growing gap between "the progressive use of digital media outside of the classroom, and the no-frills offerings of most public schools that educate our most vulnerable populations. This gap contributes to widespread alienation from educational institutions, particularly for non-dominant youth." The result is that many of these teens drop out of school or graduate without the skills needed to pursue higher-educational opportunities or find high-paying jobs. In 2010, 8% of African American teens, 15.1% of Hispanic teens, and 12.4% of Native American teens dropped out of high school as compared to 5.1% of white teens. The national unemployment rate for African Americans stands at 15.9%, 15.2% for Native Americans, and 11.5% for Latinos. In some metropolitan communities, the African American unemployment rate is three times the white rate, and the Latino unemployment rate is twice the white rate. Approximately 27.7% of all African American persons, 26.6% of all Hispanic persons (of any race), and 24.8% of Native Americans live in poverty as compared to 9.9% of all non-Hispanic white persons. School and public libraries, acting as connected learning centers, must support these adolescents who otherwise lack opportunity. They can do this by capitalizing on digital and networked media, but by also building on traditional areas of strength associated with library services for and with teens, namely:

- Support for self-directed, learner-centered inquiry
- Sanctioned intergenerational contact centered on youth interest discovery
- Safe public spaces for youth
- Strong ties to non-dominant communities/families

All school and public libraries serving teens can improve their services even more by:

- Tapping expert human resources from communities (both real and virtual)
- Connecting to school and workplace trajectories.[2]

Connecting with local schools, youth-serving organizations, after-school programs, and so on can assist public libraries in planning and implementing programs that help teens prepare for life after high school.

Teen programming is important, but let's face it—it can be time-consuming for libraries with a small staff. Therefore, it is key that libraries focus first and foremost on providing programs that are needed most by teens in the community. What are those programs? They are those that help teens succeed in school and prepare for life after high school, including transitioning to being an independent adult, attending college or other post–high school training, and pursuing a career. Typical programs that libraries provide to address these issues include the following:

- Homework help and tutoring sessions
- Projects that build research and digital-literacy skills
- Summer reading and learning programs
- Life skills workshops

---

2. Braun et al., *The Future of Library Services for and with Teens.*

- Career exploration activities
- College-readiness programs

Exactly which of these your library will focus on depends on your community assessment—once your know what programs other organizations are already providing as well as what teens' most pressing needs are, you can pare down the list above. Additionally, it's also essential to tap into community resources to help you plan, implement, and evaluate programs. There is no reason to try and do it all yourself—your community is full of people who care about youth. You just need to tap into those people and recruit them to help you implement the library's teen programs. This chapter will lay out the basics of programming for and with teens, including some sample program ideas, a section on teen summer reading and learning programs, and checklists for use in helping you to plan and implement programs. In addition to the resources and information presented in this chapter, be sure to read through YALSA's forthcoming "Teen Programming Guidelines," which will be posted at http://www.ala.org/yalsa/guidelines in early 2015.

IDENTIFYING A FOCUS FOR PROGRAMS

Multiple studies have shown that teens are leaving school unprepared for college and twenty-first-century careers. This has led to a troubling and growing problem known as "disconnected youth." There are approximately 6 million young adults who are neither in school nor working at a job. Libraries can play a key role in helping prepare teens for life after high school by offering a range of programs that help teens build life skills and that prepare them for college and careers. As a result, the library will be directly contributing to the health of the community because it is ensuring that the next generation of citizens can become informed, productive individuals who actively contribute to the community.

A first step in determining where to focus your limited resources on programming for and with teens is to determine what the biggest need is. Do research to find out about other agencies in the community that offer programs for teens and the focus of their programs. A good resource is the "Map My Community" tool on the *Find Youth Info* website (www. findyouthinfo.gov/maps/map-my-community). Just put in your zip code to find out what youth-focused programs are being offered in your community. Once you have a good handle on what other groups are doing, use this information as well as teen feedback to identify gaps in the community. For example, the local Boys and Girls Club may run a successful homework help program, and the Parks and Recreation Department often provides fun activities like crafting. You know from surveying teens in the community that there is a need for teens to build life skills so they can move toward an independent adulthood. With this information, you can focus your programs on topics like financial literacy, job interviewing techniques, cooking skills, and more.

EXAMPLES OF COMMUNITY GROUPS
THAT PROVIDE TEEN PROGRAMS

- After-School All-Stars
- After-school programs (can be at schools, community centers, religious organizations, and neighborhood associations)
- Boys and Girls Clubs of America
- Boy Scouts and Girl Scouts
- Campfire USA
- 4-H Clubs
- Girls, Inc.
- Immigrant organizations
- Museums
- Parks and Recreation Departments
- Police Athletic Leagues
- Religious organizations
- Social service agencies
- Summer camps
- Youth-focused organizations and nonprofits

PLANNING

Planning any program follows the same basic steps. Once you master those, planning and delivering teen programs becomes easier. The following program elements may apply more or less to your situation, depending on the type of program you're putting together:

- Identify the primary organizer/coordinator
- Create a brief description of the program
- Identify the purpose/goal(s) of the program
- Identify the learning outcomes (what knowledge or skill do you want teens to gain?)
- Choose a location, date, and time
- Identify the target audience and estimated attendance
- Round up partners or co-sponsors
- Identify what role—formal or informal—teens will play in planning and implementing the program
- Create a budget, taking into consideration
- Speakers' expenses (fee, travel, meals, other)
  - Supplies and equipment (materials, purchases, rentals, other)
  - Refreshments (including paper products)
  - Collection development (books and other materials to support/ enhance the program)
  - Staff time (organizer's hours × wage, PR staff hours × wage)
  - Public relations (flyers, poster, bookmarks, press releases, mailings, postage)
  - Swag (prizes, incentives, giveaways, door prizes)
  - Other costs (e.g., security or police for traffic detail)
- Identify a funding source, such as
  - Budget-line general revenue
  - Grant funds
  - Friends of the Library
  - Corporate sponsorship
  - Outside donations
  - Other
- Obtain any necessary approvals from a supervisor, library director, etc.

- Make a list of needed equipment and supplies (make arrangements to rent any, if necessary)
- Identify and confirm any speakers, presenters, or facilitators, and take care of related tasks, such as executing contracts, sending directions to the event, etc.
- Determine what the room setup will be and who will be responsible for ensuring it is ready for the event, and discuss in advance with any maintenance staff
- Determine whether there will be refreshments and who is responsible for them
- Plan for publicity and promotion, and decide who is responsible for activities such as
  o Publicity materials translated into predominant language(s) of community members
  o All library staff informed and encouraged to support the effort
  o Program information posted to library website, Facebook page, at circulation desk, etc.
  o Flyers distributed to schools, community groups, homeschoolers, businesses, and other libraries
  o Media releases to local newspapers, school papers, radio, TV, Friends of the Library newsletter, etc.
  o Visits to schools or community groups planned and approved
  o Book displays set up
  o E-mails, tweets and/or direct mailings to teens, parents, schools, and community organizations
  o Community VIPs invited (elected officials, policy makers, Foundation staff, etc.)
- Plan for accompanying resources, as appropriate, such as exhibits, displays, handouts, bibliographies, etc., and determine who is responsible for making them
- Determine how best the program can be used as a tool to raise awareness about the library by taking such actions as
  o Invite local officials, policy makers, and/or VIPs to attend
  o Recruit a local official, policy maker, and/or VIP to participate in the event (judge a contest, emcee the event, give a brief speech, etc.)
  o Other

FINAL PROGRAM CHECKLIST

____ Room setup completed

____ Volunteers/staff helpers/TAB prepped and assigned tasks

____ Equipment and supplies ready

____ Refreshments procured

____ Speaker's introduction prepared

____ Speaker's check/stipend on hand, if appropriate

____ Evaluation form and pencils available

____ Flyers for next program available

____ Parking lot details worked out

____ Someone assigned to take photos

____ Accommodations made for any special needs participants

____ Evaluation tools and method determined and any necessary surveys, etc., are created

____ Other: _____

FOLLOW-UP CHECKLIST

____ Room cleanup

____ Event photos and/or summary posted online and sent to local paper

____ Dated/time-sensitive promotional posters, etc., taken down in library and removed from website

____ Thank-you notes sent to volunteers, key staff, speaker, sponsors, etc.

____ Evaluation forms collected and analyzed

____ Debrief with key staff, supervisor, and TAG

____ Evaluation completed and results shared with coworkers, supervisor, and stakeholders

____ Other: _____

EVALUATION

It's important to take the time to determine whether or not the learning outcomes were met as well as to evaluate the process and to see where improvements can be made. Questions to ask yourself include the following:

- Was the program a success? Why or why not?
- To what degree were the learning outcomes met?
- What impact did this program have (on participants, on the community, on the library)?
- What was the estimated attendance?
- Did you encounter any unforeseen problems? How can we better prepare in the future?
- What future recommendations or best practices do you want to share?

You'll also want to share the data you collect as a means of demonstrating to your supervisor, library trustees, community members, and so on the value that the program provided to teens in the community. Sharing a mix of data and stories can help build a complete picture of what the program accomplished. Resources that can help you evaluate programs and measure outcomes can be found at the end of this chapter.

FINDING INSPIRATION FOR TEEN PROGRAMS

While there is no magic formula that can make every teen program you design a success, doing due diligence and having persistence, creativity, and a desire to try new things help considerably. There are many books that deal with programming in greater depth than we can here; for those titles, please refer to the Works Cited at the end of the chapter. If you are jumping into program design for the first time, the process might seem overwhelming. Program design isn't necessarily a matter of always coming up with amazing and creative ideas yourself, but of being tuned in to current events and leveraging existing community resources so you don't have to re-create the wheel. Good places to look identify topics for programs include the following:

1. Teens

The best way to get program ideas is from teens in your community. Go where teens gather and ask them about their interests. Be sure to seek out teens who do not normally come to the library and get their feedback. Collect information either through a formal survey or informal observation. Parents, teachers, after-school providers, and others who interact with teens regularly can also be a good source of information. If your library has teen volunteers, poll them about what kind of programs they'd like to see in the library.

2. Online Resources

The Internet is a vast repository of ideas and resources that could inform your program planning. Visit websites that offer youth-focused programs, such as 4-H, which has comprehensive ready-to-use STEM curricula on a range of topics. Each curriculum guide is about $10–15. You might also check out YALSA's "Webinars on Demand" (http://www.ala.org/yalsa/onlinelearning/webinars/webinarsondemand) for inspiration, or subscribe to e-mail lists as well, where you can solicit ideas or share your own, such as YA-YAAC@lists.ala.org.

3. Books

As we've mentioned, there are some excellent books specifically about programming for and with teens. Those books are listed on pages 86-88. Your own library's collection can also provide program inspiration. Keep up-to-date with new or popular nonfiction titles focusing on activities that teens have expressed an interest in. Check which fiction titles and series are most popular at your library, and consider offering themed programs. For example, if *The Hunger Games* is trending, teens might enjoy a program related to the movie, such as learning about wilderness survival.

4. Other Librarians and Library Staff/Local Schools

Librarians and library workers are creative people and, in general, love to share. When you visit another community, swing by the library and pick up their calendar of programs. Connect through social media and

ALA e-mail lists.[3] Attend local, regional, or national conferences, such as YALSA's annual YA Services Symposium, and exchange ideas with your peers. Even other employees in your building or library system might have great ideas or a skill you could use for a program. Contact the local schools and discuss what the trends are in technology and job-related skills for teens.

5. Youth-Focused Organizations

There are many youth-focused organizations out there that host national events and provide local organizations with free or inexpensive turn-key materials you can use to create a local event. These are great opportunities for small-staffed libraries and libraries with busy staff, because the materials are already created for you. Here are just a few examples of teen-friendly events that your library could participate in

- Banned Books Week
- Digital Learning Day
- Global Youth Service Day
- Hour of Code
- Library Card Sign-Up Month
- Lights on Afterschool
- Mozilla's Maker Party
- Read Across America
- Summer Learning Day
- Teen Read Week™
- Teen Tech Week™

Each of these initiatives provides free materials online that libraries can access and adapt for themselves for use with planning and carrying out a local celebration or event.

---

3. To subscribe to ALA mailing lists, log in at "ALA Electronic Discussion Lists," http://lists.ala.org/sympa.

IDENTIFYING INDIVIDUALS WHO CAN HELP WITH PROGRAMMING

Remember that you don't have to do it all yourself or be the expert of everything! Look for community members who are passionate about helping youth, and recruit them to help you plan and implement programs or serve as speakers, coaches, mentors, or facilitators. Possibilities include the following:

- Business owners
- College and graduate students
- Faculty at local colleges
- Library coworkers
- Museum staff
- Parents of teens
- Retirees
- Scout leaders
- Social services workers
- Staff at other youth-serving organizations
- Teachers
- Teens

Start building a contacts list of potential program presenters, facilitators, et cetera, and add to it as you meet people in the community. Ask individuals whom you trust for recommendations. Think about what sort of information or training they might need in order to have successful interactions with teens, and work to provide that via a conference call, meeting, or handbook. Advocates for Youth and 4-H both provide resources about facilitating adult-youth partnerships that you can adapt for use with your library.

SUMMER READING AND LEARNING[4]

Because public libraries have a long tradition of providing learning activities for youth when school is not in session, it's worth taking the time

---

4. For a quick introduction to summer reading, see YALSA, *The Complete Summer Reading Program Manual: From Planning to Evaluation* (Chicago: YALSA, 2012).

here to go into some detail about summer reading/learning programs for and with teens. Your library probably already offers a summer reading and learning program for youth. Summer programs are a service for the community—offering youth encouragement to continue reading and learning during the summer. Teens, though some have jobs or take classes in the summer, also need the same encouragement as well as somewhere safe to go. A summer reading and learning program can be a big investment of time and planning, but it can lay the foundation for teen involvement during the rest of the year and also bring in new patrons. If you are designing a summer reading/learning program for teens for the first time, look at the following checklist:

1. Planning

What are your expected outcomes? Do you want teens to learn a new skill, maintain current literacy levels, something else? Decide how you will measure whether or not you achieved the goal. Libraries typically track outputs, like number of pages read or number of participants. However, libraries also need to track outcomes, such as what knowledge or skills teens gained. You can do this via pre- and post-surveys of participants, focus groups, program evaluations, and more.

2. Tracking Progress:

In order to know whether or not your summer reading/learning program is achieving its stated goals, you'll need to gather a variety of data. Things like pre- and post-surveys of teen patrons or their parents, on-the-spot evaluation sheets at the close of programs, focus groups, and more are all methods you could use. One option is a tracking sheet, which is a tool that is portable, easy to use at a glance, and durable. Examples of teen summer reading/learning tracking cards can be found at the end of this chapter. Formats and sizes are variable depending on convenience for your teen patrons:

- Business card
- Pocket-size trifold
- Digital tracking options

Resources that can help you track progress and measure outcomes can also be found at the end of this chapter.

3. Rewards

Sometimes young people are more motivated to learn when there is a competition or prize. Consider offering rewards for different levels of activities, to facilitate broad participation:

- Easy
  - "Liking" the library Facebook page
  - Asking a librarian or library worker for a book recommendation
  - Checking out a type of media you want to spotlight: video games, playaways, magazines, etc.
- Moderate
  - Participating in programs and bringing friends
  - Creating a book review
- Advanced
  - Achieving a reading goal
  - Using or remixing library e-content in a learning project

Rewarding activities like these promotes library services that teens may not be familiar with and also encourages participation from kids who "don't read."

There are several considerations when you think of summer reading/learning prizes and incentives. For example, rewards can be given in many different ways:

- Small prizes can be given out at standard points along the road to completion—e.g., after reading for a certain number of hours, a teen gets a certain prize.
- Teens can get a larger prize for finishing the entire reading program or a particular project—reading a certain number of total hours, or finishing a certain number of activities. This prize can be given out in addition to other prizes along the way.

- You can offer a grand prize that only a few randomly selected participants will win. Popular prizes include iPads and iPods, e-readers, video game systems, bikes, and high-value gift certificates.
- Prizes can be "gamified"—teens get points for reading and gaining new skills, and they choose when and how to spend them. The prizes are assigned certain point values.

Prizes can come from a variety of sources. If your prize budget is very limited, approach local businesses for coupons, gift certificates, and overstock merchandise. Often a "buy one/get one free" approach is especially effective, as this provides the local businesses some free advertising. Whatever prizes you are thinking of offering, talk about them with your teen volunteers, or consider polling teens in your community to gauge their popularity.

4. Programs

Teen summer reading/learning involves programming—the capacity of your library will determine the frequency. Teen summer reading/learning events should be diverse, so as to appeal to a wide range of people and to provide a variety of activities.

- *Performances:* These programs could be more expensive than others depending on the performer, but you don't have to do as much of the work. Think outside the box with performers, and, again, tap your community. Think about audience involvement when looking for performers for teens. Passivity forms a large part of teens' experience of school and entertainment, and libraries offer the chance for something interactive. Programs of this type can include the following:
  o Plays or improv sessions performed by local theater groups
  o Performances by local musicians
  o Dance performances
  o Poetry slams led by local poets

Of course, the actual type of programs will vary based on the needs and interests of teens in your community.

- *Workshops:* These educational sessions help teens gain specific skills and can be "one and done" sessions that teach a particular skill, such as how to build a bookshelf; or, for more in-depth learning on a broad topic, can be organized into a series of workshops spread out over days or weeks. For example, your library could offer a series of STEM-focused workshops that expose teens to a range of possible careers in science, technology, engineering, or math. Be sure to focus the topics on the needs and interests of teens and involve them in the planning. And don't forget that you don't have to be the expert—tap community volunteers to run the workshops.

- *Crafts and DIY:* Summer is also a time for teens to unwind and pursue fun hobbies in a safe and welcoming space. Many teens enjoy making things and learning new skills. Find out if other community organizations are offering craft or DIY programs, and be sure not to replicate what's already being done. One important consideration for a successful craft program is having clear instructions. Be sure that the program leader tests them and demonstrate them to others. Be sure to proactively address safety concerns with crafts that involve potentially dangerous tools such as craft knives, hot-glue guns, irons, and so on, by having stated guidelines/instructions for safe use, ensuring adequate adult supervision, and demonstrating proper use before permitting teen patrons to handle the tools.

- *Multigenerational:* For libraries with a small staff, creating programming that engages multiple age groups can be a time- and resource-saving device, but also a way to bring different parts of the community together. Teen patrons can lead storytimes for toddlers and other youngsters. Intergenerational book groups can lead to richer discussions and broader perspectives, but also expose teens to positive role models and give adults a chance to give back to the community by volunteering some time with teens. Today's teens are digital natives and can be a great resource for helping senior citizens learn how to do things like set up a Facebook page so they can keep in touch with grandchildren, digitize photos, start a blog, and more.

- *Clubs:* These are recurring meetings of teens who share similar interests, the topics of which are limited only by the interests of teens in your community. These clubs can be led by teens or by a community volunteer with special interest or expertise on the topic. Clubs can be organized for social, educational, or recreational purposes. For example, some teens in your community might be interested in a robotics club that brings together people who are interested in learning about, building, and showing off their own robots.
- *Passive:* These do-on-your-own-time activities are great for libraries with limited staff and resources, as well as for communities where teens are either busy with other responsibilities or have trouble coming regularly to the library. These could involve writing and submitting book reviews, designing a bookmark, completing a scavenger hunt, and other activities. Think about how you can leverage the library's website for passive programs.
- *Parties:* Parties are a way to celebrate teens and their contributions to the library. They can be great at the beginning of the program as a marketing tool, or at the end of the summer to celebrate teen achievements. Parties are limited only by the library's resources and the interests of teen patrons. Some examples of party activities include the following:
  - o Gaming
  - o Carnival games like ring toss, bowling, etc.
  - o Pizza or ice cream parties
  - o Themed activities, such as a spy party with a code-breaking challenge
  - o "Gallery openings" to show off teen artwork or other projects
  - o "Book launch" parties to unveil and celebrate teen writing projects

EVALUATION AND WRAP-UP

It's important to take the time to determine whether or not the learning outcomes were met as well as to evaluate the overall summer reading/ learning program and to see where improvements can be made for next year. Questions to ask yourself include the following:

- Was the program a success? Why or why not?
- To what degree were the learning outcomes met?
- What impact did this program have (on participants, on the community, on the library)?
- What was the estimated attendance?
- Did you encounter any unforeseen problems? How can we better prepare in the future?
- What future recommendations or best practices do you want to share?

You'll also want to share the data you collect as a means of demonstrating to your supervisor, library trustees, community members, and so on the value that the program provided to the teens in the community. Be aware that many state library agencies expect libraries to collect certain data and submit it to them at the end of the summer. Sharing a mix of data and stories can help build a complete picture of how the summer reading/learning program helped prevent the summer slide in teens who participated in library activities. Resources that can help you evaluate programs and measure outcomes can be found at the end of this chapter.

TEEN-LED PROGRAMMING

As explored in the webinar "Collaborating with Teens to Build Better Library Programs" by Jennifer Velasquez, when teens design and lead programs, they can have more commitment to the event and be more invested in its success. In chapter 7, we talk a little about letting teen volunteers direct and design programs, but you can engage in teen-led programming without having a teen volunteer group at all. Consider having a free-form teen night, where you provide a variety of supplies, games, and maybe a few ideas, but the teens themselves are the ones who decide what they'll do.

A Librarian Shares Her Experience
with Teen-Led Programming

"I'd wanted to try teen-driven programs and the ALA webinar 'Collaborating with Teens to Build Better Library Programs' by Jennifer Velasquez ignited me to begin.

Teen-driven library programs empower teens by using the active energy of the moment to choose and implement the evening's program. This approach also gives teens ownership and responsibility. Once in a while I would need to clarify that while I have lots of ideas and creativity, this is your program: What do you want to do this evening? I keep random supplies that can be used for open-ended multiple purposes. More than one activity can take place in the same room. One night some teens were creating with LEGOS while others crafted duct-tape wallets and phone cases, and a few others were on their laptops writing stories. Video games, card games, and board games were available, with some teens bringing games from their personal collections as well as making use of the library's resources.

This model also allows for pre-planned programs, if that is the consensus [of the teens]. A cohesive, flexible framework develops through collaboration . While providing a strong social component, teen-driven programs utilize creativity and support autonomy."

—Kathy Kearney
Pueblo City-County Library District

MARKETING AND PROMOTION

Even the most exciting program is of no use if no one shows up. Increasing program attendance gets more teens in the library and increases the visibility of the library in the community—all primary goals of many libraries! Increasing program participation owes as much to good marketing as to good design, but most library staff aren't trained in marketing. Here are some suggestions for places to start:

The Schools

Sometimes it's hard to find out where teens are in your community, but there is one place most of them attend almost every day—school. There are many ways to get your message into the schools:

- Connect with the school librarian to find out what they recommend is the best way to market library programs to students. Offer to reciprocate.
- If you are visiting a school for any reason or are leading a library tour for a school group, advertise your next program with gusto. Create a flyer to leave behind.
- Many schools have packets they send home with announcements or regular newsletters. Contact the school to get your program information into these.
- If you have one, talk to your library's Community Relations department about getting a comprehensive brochure listing the library's teen events. Talk to the schools about putting it in the library, in teachers' mailboxes, or just at the front desk.
- Take programs on the road to an after-school group. Bring along information about your other upcoming library programs.
- Participate in freshman orientation at high schools, and give teens information about library programs.

Word of Mouth

As we will discuss in chapter 7, a Teen Advisory Board or regular teen volunteer group can form the backbone of teen programming with members spreading the word to their friends. If teens are a part of the program design process, they are even more likely to advertise the program to their peers. Don't be afraid to mention your programs to patrons whom you interact with in the course of your daily reference interactions, either.

Community Partners

As we will discuss in chapter 9, partnering with other community organizations can be a great way to promote your events to their audiences. For example, if you are arranging a cooking class, find out if there's a cooking school in the community or if cooking is taught at a technical/vocational college. If other organizations are involved in the event, they will promote it to their constituents and get your message out to a broader audience. If you are having a Free Comic Book Day celebration, include local comic shops in the planning and ask them to help promote the event. They'll talk to their customers about it—especially if they have a stake in the event.

EXAMPLES OF PROGRAMS

Don't forget that the focus of your programs will depend on the needs and interests of teens in your community. Listed below are some sample program ideas that may or may not fit the particular needs of your community, but they can help give you a picture of what other libraries are doing.

Technology

Technology programs are great for introducing teens of all skill levels to new tools and for teaching new skills in a fun way.

- *Video Game Design:* Tools like GameMaker, Gamestar Mechanic, Scratch, Kodu, and Unreal Development Kit[5] help teens and tweens make their own video games. Find a person in the community or

---

5. GameMaker Studio (Yoyo Games, Ltd., 2013), http://www.yoyogames.com/studio; Gamestar Mechanic (E-Line Media and Institute of Play), http://gamestarmechanic.com/; Scratch (Lifelong Kindergarten Group at the MIT Media Lab), http://scratch.mit.edu/; Kodu Game Lab (Microsoft Research), http://www.kodugamelab.com/; Unreal Development Kit (Epic Games, Inc., 2014), http://www.unrealengine.com/udk/.

on your staff who is comfortable with the system to organize the program. Video game design teaches teens about visual design, problem solving, communication skills, and more. Consider hosting a contest for the best game.[6]

- *Digital Filmmaking:* From the basics of storyboarding, lighting, and editing to makeup, stage combat, and digital effects, filmmaking workshops inspire and excite. Look for local filmmakers to help lead one. These could be teens, teachers at the local school, or an instructor at a local college. Consider hosting a film festival or screening! If the teens enjoy making films, they can even film other programs to help promote the library. Filmmaking helps teens learn about storytelling while also getting hands-on experience with digital tools that can help them in jobs.

- *Electronics and Computer Programming:* Arduino[7] is a wonderful, accessible system that can be used to make things such as real clothes that react to gestures, self-watering plant pots, and doorknobs that only open to specific coded knocks. Teens learn about coding, circuitry, and more through use of these kits. Arduino or Raspberry Pi[8] sets are not free, but many grants support youth technology learning. Tap a teen who's a tech guru or ask for volunteers from a local electronics store like Best Buy to coordinate the program.

Gaming

Almost everyone loves games. Role-play, strategy, shooting, or dance—there's a game for everyone. Gaming helps teens gain a variety of key soft skills like teamwork, conflict management, time management, precision, problem solving, and more.

---

6. A great contest opportunity for young game designers is the STEM Video Game Challenge: National STEM Video Game Challenge (Joan Ganz Cooney Center, 2014), http://www.stemchallenge.org/.
7. For more information on Arduino and associated products, check out http://www.arduino.cc/.
8. A Raspberry Pi is essentially a miniaturized computer hard drive, similar to an Arduino but with unique capabilities. Find more information on Raspberry Pi at http://www.raspberrypi.org/.

- *Video Games:* Borrow a gaming system or purchase one for the library, if your budget allows, and put in multiplayer games that are popular with teens. Host themed contests like retro-gaming, racing games, or dance games, or just play. If your teen patrons are interested, consider setting up an educational Minecraft account.[9] Minecraft is not only a game that young people enjoy playing; it also teaches them how to code.
- *Tabletop Games:* Bring out the board games and role-playing games and go to town! Teens can bring their favorites, or you can request leaders and demos from local stores.[10]
- *Special Games:* Get creative. Make giant board games, live-action versions of video games, or whatever ideas your teen volunteers come up with. Consider converting your parking lot into a giant chess board with teens as live pieces!

The Arts

Teens often experiment with creative expression, and library art programs are a great way to introduce teens to new techniques, as well as to celebrate their work. Art-focused programs encourage soft skills like inquisitiveness, self-confidence, flexibility, and more.

- *Writing:* What better place to explore writing than at a library? Bring in local poets, authors, and creative-writing professors to lead sessions on different kinds of writing—long and short, poetry and prose.
- *Slam Poetry:* Slam poetry is a both a form of writing and a form of performance. Look into getting local slam poets to lead a group or host a performance at the library. Need to find a poet? Browse a list of poets on the Poetry Foundation's website: www.poetryfoundation.org/browse/poets.

9. More information on getting an educational Minecraft account can be found at MinecraftEdu (Teacher Gaming LLC), http://minecraftedu.com/.
10. If you like board games, consider taking part in International Games Day: International Games Day @ Your Library, http://igd.ala.org/.

- *Writing Clubs:* If your library has a lot of teen patrons who like to write, consider hosting a weekly or monthly club where they can share their work and help one another. Find a volunteer in the community who can host the club, such as a retired teacher or local author.
- *Contests and Passive Programs:* Writing lends itself to the passive program format, because it doesn't have to happen in the library. Pick a theme or style, such as the short story, and create and distribute a form to gather teen submissions. Tap into local VIPs, such as town council members, to serve as judges. Winning entries can be collected in a book, posted on the library website, or even printed large and exhibited in your library.
- *NaNoWriMo*[11]: National Novel Writing Month (held in November) challenges participants to write an entire novel in only thirty days. Are your teen patrons up for the challenge?

Visual Art

Visual art programs help teen art find an audience, and the library is a wonderful, free space to exhibit teen art.

- *Spray Paint Art:* Get some cans of spray paint and a few large canvases, Masonite boards, or sheets, and let teens create to their hearts' content. Often paint stores and hardware stores will be willing to donate paint or other supplies. Find a local artist or art teacher who can share some techniques with the teens. This program requires caution and a large outdoor space!
- *Comic Art or Manga Drawing:* Teens themselves often have the skill to lead these workshops, or contact a local writer, artist, or art teacher. Results lend themselves well to exhibition and compilation.
- *Collaborative Mural Making:* Whether you want to use paint and canvas or paper and markers, challenge a group of teens to create a work of art together. This program can be as organized or as free-form as you like.

---

11. For more information on NaNoWriMo, check out the official website: National Novel Writing Month, http://nanowrimo.org/.

Performance

Give teens the spotlight. These are great programs to film for virtual exhibition—especially if the filmmakers are also teens!

- *Improv Club:* Funny and unexpected, improvisation is a great way for teens to get to know each other and have fun—and typically at a very low cost!
- *Readers' Theater:* Without the pressure of costumes and memorization, readers' theater can be a great introduction to acting for teens who would normally be too shy. Teen performers can present to younger children for benefits to all!
- *Interactive Mysteries*[12]: Often mysteries activities are available as kits and can be ordered online.[13] Your teen patrons may enjoy creating one themselves!
- *Original Plays:* Teens may like to have the opportunity to write, direct, and perform their own plays. This is a great opportunity to team up with a local drama troupe or drama teacher. You might be amazed at what develops!

ON THE LIGHTER SIDE: PROGRAMS-IN-A-BOX

Following are easy programs-in-a-box that can be made into kits, saved, and used at different locations.

Duct Tape Extravaganza[14]

The focus of this craft program is to provide a fun and easy way for teens to be creative. This is the number-one most popular program-in-a-box at the Pueblo City-County Library, beloved by teens and tweens alike.

---

12. Check out this guide to running interactive mysteries: Karen Siwak, *Library Programming for Teens: Mystery Theater (VOYA Guides)* (Lanham, MD: Scarecrow Press, 2010).
13. A resource used by many libraries is Janet Dickey, "Anyone's Guess Mystery Program Kits for Teens," JanetDickey.com, http://janetdickey.com/teen-kits.php.
14. New duct tape crafts are developed and posted online all the time, so stay up-to-date with the following websites: "Ducktivities," *Duck Tape* (ShurTech Brands, LLC., 2013), http://duckbrand.com/duck-tape-club/ducktivities; "Craft Projects Using Duct Tape," *Cut Out + Keep* (Cut Out + Keep, 2014), http://www.cutoutandkeep.net/projects/using/duct_tape. Other good websites to search for tutorials include Instructables, YouTube, and Pinterest.

Supplies

- Duct tape: gray, colored, and patterned. Get more than you think you will need.
- Box cutters and X-Acto knives: I find that scissors get too gummy to cut duct tape effectively
- Jewelry supplies (optional): earring hooks, clasps, etc.
- Felt and other fabric (optional): for duct tape phone cases

Instructions

There are many options for duct tape crafts, and many teens already know how to make at least one of these:

- Wallets
- Earrings
- Bracelets
- Roses
- Phone cases

To make earrings:

Tear off two strips of tape, and lay one on top of the other, sticky sides together. Trace a shape on the tape—hearts, feathers, or whatever else you choose. Your earrings can match, but they don't have to! Cut the shapes out carefully, and pierce a small hole in each one. Thread the earring hooks through the holes, tightening them, if necessary, with a set of pliers.

Freezer Paper Stenciling

This program-in-a-box is another way to allow teens to explore their creative side, and it easily adapts itself to many book and movie release parties.

Supplies

- Freezer paper
- X-Acto knives
- Stencils: these can be found online and printed out directly onto the freezer paper, or teens can draw their own designs

- Fabric paint
- Sponge brushes
- T-shirts or bandannas: unless the patrons are expected to bring their own
- An iron and ironing board

Instructions

If using a printer, cut freezer paper into 8.5" × 11" rectangles, or another printer-compatible size, and print your design on the dull side of the paper. Teens can always draw designs of their own as well. Cut the design out carefully with an X-Acto knife. Fuse the freezer paper to the fabric with a hot, dry iron, shiny-side down—many brands of freezer paper include instructions for this process on the box. If you are using a T-shirt, insert a plastic bag after ironing so that the paint doesn't bleed through. Sponge paint onto the fabric evenly, let dry, and carefully peel off the paper. Use the iron to heat-set the paint before taking your creation home.

Minute to Win It[15]

Harness the spirit of competition among your teens in order to teach them teamwork, working well under pressure, communication skills, self-confidence, and other soft skills. This is also a good activity to use if your teen patrons have been sitting for a while and need to burn off some energy. Organize teens into groups who compete with one another at specific challenges. A dozen potential challenges follow, but you can find more online if you wish.

- *Battle Rattle:* Place marbles inside two inverted water bottles taped together. Shake to get the marbles from one bottle to the other.
- *Back Flip:* In increments of two, place pencils on the back of your hand and then flip them off and catch all of them. Can you get up to twelve?

---

15. Many of these activities are adapted from activities from the official show web page: *Minute to Win It*, NBC.com, http://www.nbc.com/minute-to-win-it/.

- *Breakfast Scramble:* Assemble the front of a cereal box that has been cut into pieces.
- *Caddy Stack:* Stack three golf balls one atop the other. This requires a very level surface!
- *Elephant March:* Knock over bottles with a baseball hanging from panty hose worn on your head. Make sure other contestants stay out of the way for this challenge!
- *Face the Cookie:* Using only your face, move cookies from your forehead to your mouth.
- *Junk in the Trunk:* Wiggle a box full of Ping-Pong balls attached to your waist until it is empty.
- *Nose-Dive:* Transfer as many cotton balls as possible, one at a time, from one serving bowl to another using only petroleum jelly on your nose.
- *Tilt-a-Cup:* Bounce a Ping-Pong ball off the ground with one hand, and catch it in a cup held in the other. Each time you catch a Ping-Pong ball, stack a new cup on top of it and try to catch another. The object of this challenge is to make the highest cup stack you can in one minute.
- *Skittle Scurry:* Set a large bowl of Skittles at one side of the table and a cup on the other side. Transfer as many Skittles from the bowl to the cup using only a straw and the natural power of suction.
- *Balloon Head:* Keep an inflated balloon in the air using only your head—do not touch the balloon with your hands, feet, or any other body part.
- *Book Balance:* Walk a determined distance while balancing a book on your head. Every time you turn around, another book is added to the stack. How high can you make the stack?

I recommend testing these challenges before the program to check the difficulty level—or have your teen volunteers test them! As a bonus, most of the supplies for this program are fairly inexpensive.

T-Shirt Hacks

Let teens show off their creative side! T-shirts can be used to make everything from bags, scarves, toys, and rugs.

Supplies
- Old T-shirts: These are generally easy to get from your colleagues, patrons, or thrift stores. You may want to wash them before the program.
- Scissors
- Fabric glue
- Needles and thread
- Accessories (optional, depends on your plans): buttons, snaps, zippers, etc.
- Fabric paint (optional)
- Sewing machine (optional)

Instructions
There are many, many possible ways to remake a T-shirt, but here's a quick, easy example.

T-shirt Tote Bag:
Cut off both sleeves of the shirt, inside the shoulder seams. Cut the neck into a gentle arc. The neck becomes the top opening of your tote; the two straps left from the shoulders become the tote's handles. Now you just have to seal the bottom, which can be achieved in a few ways.

- Snip a hole in the inside of the bottom seam of the shirt. Thread a drawstring through the seam, gathering up the bottom of the shirt as you go. Pull tight and tie securely.
- Cut the bottom of your shirt into a regularly spaced fringe, making sure to cut through the front and back layers evenly. Tie each pair of front and back fringe strips together to seal the bottom of the shirt.
- You can always sew the bottom closed, either by hand, or by machine.

The great thing about T-shirt crafts is that there are options for all skill levels, so make sure to include simple, no-sew projects as well as more complicated projects. This is a craft that can appeal to boys as well as girls.

LIBRARIANS' CONTRIBUTIONS

What program has been your most popular?

"Our DIY Teen program is insanely popular! We had 29 teens at one, but usually have 20, and never fewer than 16. Every week, Tuesdays at two, we host a new craft program. We give them examples of the finished product, and give a tutorial on how to make their own, but we encourage them to be creative."

What unique or original programs have you hosted at your library?

"We are hosting a trivia program in the winter, and all of the questions are coming from_freerice.com so that for every correct answer, ten grains of rice are donated to a hungry person somewhere in the world. We are accepting donations for our local food banks at this family trivia event."

Have you ever made a Program-in-a-Box?

"For the Hunger Games movie release last year, I hosted a Cornucopia Challenge at three branches (http://www.bethanymediacenter.com/Cornucopia-Challenge.html). I guess it could be considered a program-in-a-box since it was the same thing that traveled between branches."

What creative ways do you advertise programs?

"We make up quarter-sheet flyers for programs or contests (film, short story, battle of the bands) and tape them to the side of the PCs in the Teen area. That way they can't help but know what programs we offer!"

—April Shroeder, MLS
Teen Services Librarian
Gum Spring Library
Loudoun County Public Library, Virginia

ON PROGRAMS-IN-A-BOX

"We have 28 individual kits, that range from a Wii gaming system and board game kits, to things like a Luau kit and a Mardi Gras Party kit. The cost really depends on the kit. Obviously the Wii kit and Guitar Hero kit cost more than some of the board game and party kits, but it's a lot less expensive to share a gaming system among libraries rather than purchasing multiples.

They are housed at different libraries throughout the system in Rubbermaid Totes, and each kit has a catalog record with an inventory of the contents. They are for staff use only, and staff are responsible for making sure that they notify our Teen Programming Committee if articles are lost or damaged. This has worked really well in our library system and is really a great way to have some programs ready at a moment's notice."

—Sarah J. Kramer
Librarian I, Youth Services
Southeast Regional Library
Garner, North Carolina

Rebecca Denham's blog, http://lunanshee.blogspot.com/, contains her favorite teen programs, but she was kind enough to provide us the detailed instructions for one of our favorites—the Anti-Valentine's Party:

Anti-Valentine's Party

Supplies
- Anti-Valentine's Day Cards
  - Craft/scrapbooking paper in blacks, reds, skull, and funerary themes
  - Glue sticks
  - Scissors
  - Black, silver, red glitter
  - Anti-Valentine's Day phrases for cards (some funny ones here and here)
    - http://girlsguideto.com/articles/best-funny-anti-valentine-s-day-quotes
    - http://www.tumblr.com/tagged/anti%20valentines%20day
- Decorations
  - Black and gray streamers and balloons (optional)
- Snacks
  - "Blackened Heart Cookies"
    - Add black food coloring to regular sugar cookies, cut into heart shapes, and bake.
    - You can also use a "broken" heart cookie cutter (www.cheapcookiecutters.com has a fun one).
- Sour Patch Kids/Strips etc.
- Drinks
    - "Heart's Blood Punch" (http://www.bhg.com/recipe/drinks/watermelon-cooler-punch/)
    - "Tainted Love Lunch" (http://www.bhg.com/recipe/drinks/pisco-sour-drink/)—replace pisco with sparkling water!

- Beating Heart Piñata
  - Buy or make a heart-shaped piñata (if making it, check out http://pinataboy.com/makeaheart.html for easy instructions)
  - Stuff with sour/bitter candies and chocolate
  - Use a broomstick wrapped in black streamers to hit piñata
- Non-Romantic or Mock-ably Romantic movie (shorter is better)
  - *Twilight, Step Up, Gremlins, Coraline, Eight Legged Freaks*, etc.
- Non-Romantic (or downright tragic) books to display/booktalk
  - *Me and Earl and the Dying Girl*, by Jesse Andrews
  - *How They Croaked: The Awful Ends of the Awfully Famous*, by Georgia Bragg and Kevin O'Malley
  - *Going Bovine*, by Libba Bray
  - *Deadline*, by Chris Crutcher
  - *Phineas Gage: A Gruesome but True Story about Brain Science*, by John Fleischman
  - *Right Behind You*, by Gail Giles
  - *The Fault in Our Stars*, by John Green
  - *Masque of the Red Death*, by Bethany Griffin
  - *Everybody Sees the Ants*, by A. S. King
  - *I Hunt Killers*, by Barry Lyga
  - *Ten*, by Gretchen McNiel
  - *I Am Not a Serial Killer*, by Dan Wells
  - *Pivot Point*, by Kasie West
  - *In the Shadow of Blackbirds*, by Cat Winters
  - *Paper Valentine*, by Brenna Yovanoff

Running the Program

Set out Anti-Valentine's Card supplies along with snacks. Play a non-romantic movie while teens are making Anti-Valentine's Cards (this year I'm showing *Eight Legged Freaks*). When the movie is finished, have teens clean up room and put up tables and chairs, then hang piñata. Have teens use broomstick to hit piñata—make sure that non-stick-swinging teens are *far back* from the piñata. Just because it's an Anti-Valentine's Day party doesn't mean they need to end up with a black eye or busted head.

—Rebecca Denham
http://lunanshee.blogspot.com/

ADDITIONAL RESOURCES

- Flowers, Sarah. *Evaluating Teen Services and Programs*. Chicago: Neal Schuman, 2012.
- IMLS. "Outcomes-Based Evaluation." http://www.imls.gov/applicants/basics.aspx.
- YALSA. *Making in the Library Toolkit: Makerspace Resources Task Force*. 2014. American Library Association. http://www.ala.org/yalsa/sites/ala.org.yalsa/files/content/MakingintheLibraryToolkit2014.pdf.
- YALSA. *STEM* Programming Toolkit (*Science, Technology, Engineering & Math)*. February 2013. www.ala.org/yalsa/sites/ala.org.yalsa/files/content/STEMtoolkit_Final_2013.docx.
- YALSA. "Teen Programming Guidelines." Chicago: YALSA, 2015. http://www.ala.org/yalsa/guidelines.
- YALSA. *The Complete Summer Reading Manual: From Planning to Evaluation*. Chicago: YALSA, 2012.
- YALSA archived webinars (accessible at www.ala.org/yalsa/webinars)
  - "Critic's Choice: Programming Ideas for Older Teens" (2013)
  - "Demonstrating Impact through Teen Summer Reading" (2013)

- o "Easy-to-Implement Teen Programs" (2013)
- o "Practical Programming Ideas for Teens" (2013)
- o "What's Next for Teen Services?" (2014)
- YALSA Web and wiki pages:
  - o "Afterschool Programs," http://wikis.ala.org/yalsa/index.php/After_School_Programs
  - o "College and Career Readiness," http://wikis.ala.org/yalsa/index.php/College_%26_Career_Readiness
  - o "Summer Reading and Learning," http://summerreading.ning.com/
  - o "Teen Read Week™," www.ala.org/teenread
  - o "Teen Tech Week™," www.ala.org/teentechweek
- YA-YAAC@lists.ala.org is an open Listserv that anyone can subscribe to. The purpose of this resource is to provide a space for library staff to share ideas and resources around teen programming. Subscribe at http://lists.ala.org/sympa.

WORKS CITED

Bowers, Sharon. *Candy Construction: How to Build Race Cars, Castles, and Other Cool Stuff Out of Store-Bought Candy*. North Adams, MA: Storey Publishing, 2010.

Braun, Linda W., Maureen L. Hartman, Sandra Hughes-Hassell, and Kafi Kumasi, with contributions from Beth Yoke. *The Future of Library Services for and with Teens: A Call to Action*. January 8, 2014. http://www.ala.org/yaforum/sites/ala.org.yaforum/files/content/YALSA_nationalforum_final.pdf.

Dickey, Janet. "Anyone's Guess Mystery Program Kits for Teens." *Janet Dickey.com*. http://janetdickey.com/teen-kits.php.

Forks, Brittany. *Kilobyte Culture: Geek Chic Jewelry to Make from Easy-to-Find Computer Components*. New York: Potter Craft, 2009.

Gerson, Fany. *Paletas: Authentic Recipes for Mexican Ice Pops, Shaved Ice and Aguas Frescas*. Berkeley, CA: Ten Speed Press, 2011.

Itoh, Makiko. *The Just Bento Cookbook: Everyday Lunches to Go*. New York: Kodansha USA, 2011. Or consult Itoh's website: *Just Bento*. http://justbento.com/.

Nicolay, Megan. *Generation T: Beyond Fashion: 120 New Ways to Transform a T-Shirt*. New York: Workman, 2009.

Nicolay, Megan. *Generation T: 108 Ways to Transform a T-Shirt*. New York: Workman, 2006. http://www.generation-t.com/.

Rogge, Hannah. *Hardwear: Jewelry from a Toolbox*. New York: Stewart, Tabori and Chang, 2006.

Siwak, Karen. *Library Programming for Teens: Mystery Theater (VOYA Guides)*. Lanham, MD: Scarecrow Press, 2010.

YALSA. *The Complete Summer Reading Program Manual: From Planning to Evaluation*. Chicago: YALSA, 2012.

YALSA, "Webinars on Demand." Young Adult Library Services Association. American Library Association, 2014. http://www.ala.org/yalsa/onlinelearning/webinars/webinarsondemand.

PROGRAMMING WEBSITES

Arduino. http://www.arduino.cc/.

"Craft Projects Using Duct Tape." Cut Out + Keep, 2014. http://www.cutoutandkeep.net/projects/using/duct_tape.

"Ducktivities." *Duck Tape*. ShurTech Brands, LLC., 2013. http://duckbrand.com/duck-tape-club/ducktivities.

Free Comic Book Day. Diamond Comic Distributors & ComicsPRO, 2014. http://www.freecomicbookday.com.

GameMaker Studio. Yoyo Games, Ltd., 2013. http://www.yoyogames.com/studio.

Gamestar Mechanic. E-Line Media and Institute of Play. http://gamestarmechanic.com/.

"How to Make a PVC Bow and Arrow." *wikiHow*. http://www.wikihow.com/Make-a-PVC-Bow-and-Arrow.

6 | Leveraging Teen Volunteers and Teen Advisory Boards to Boost your Capacity

TEENS HAVE A high rate of volunteerism; on average, 26% of teens in the United States volunteer each year,[1] and many middle and high schools, both public and private, require community service hours for graduation. Taking that 26% figure into account, a community the size of Flint, Michigan (population 101,558), could have as many as 26,000 teen volunteers!

A library is a wonderful place for teens to volunteer—a neutral space with caring adults and a trusted community entity. But hosting a teen volunteer program in your library isn't just good for teens: it's great for the library, too. Running a volunteer program helps librarians and library workers connect with teens in the community to familiarize them with the important role that libraries play in contributing to a thriving community. It can help make the library a destination for teens, rather than just a place they vaguely know exists. A successful teen volunteer program can increase teen program attendance and the visibility of the library in the community at large. In addition, many teens have skills and expertise that the libraries can benefit from, whether they're avid readers who can help select books for the teen section, or tech gurus who can help you amp up your library's website.

This chapter will provide helpful tools for those new to managing volunteer programs:

---

1. Bureau of Labor Statistics, "Volunteering in the United States, 2012," United States Department of Labor, February 22, 2013, http://www.bls.gov/news.release/archives/volun_02222013.pdf.

- A helpful guide to starting a teen volunteer program, or taking on a volunteer program that already exists.
- Guidelines for recruiting, managing, and training volunteers.
- Tips for dealing with common problems.
- Sample volunteer policies, timesheets, and application forms.
- A list of simple, recurring tasks that volunteers can take off your plate.

TEEN VOLUNTEER PROGRAMS VS. TEEN ADVISORY BOARDS

Teen Volunteer Programs and Teen Advisory Boards will be mentioned a lot in this chapter. Here are the key differences between them:

- *Volunteers:* The purpose of volunteers is to build the capacity of the library by getting extra support for the work that the library wants to achieve. Volunteers can work alone or in groups. Depending on your schedule and your library's needs, volunteers may be able to work any time the library is open. Volunteers can help with the daily work of the library or work on longer-term projects. A key to success is to tap into the expertise and interests of the individual volunteer and find a task or project that is a good fit for them.
- *Teen Advisory Boards:* The purpose of these boards is to provide a formal way to engage teens in the mission of the library and to use their input and ideas to help shape the overall teen program at the library. These groups often tend to meet at regular, specific times. Teen Advisory Boards are more directly involved in teen programs and services than basic volunteers are. The idea of a Teen Advisory Board is to give teens a stake in the library and a say in how teen services are planned, implemented, and evaluated. Teen Advisory Boards can offer feedback on things like teen space design and upkeep, program planning, and the library's summer reading/learning program. They can also work on creative, teen-led projects in the library.

WHY HAVE A TEEN VOLUNTEER PROGRAM OR TEEN ADVISORY BOARD?

Small libraries in particular suffer from a lack of human resources—there aren't enough staff to help the library achieve its mission and goals. Volunteers of any age can be tapped to help advance the work of the library; however, teen volunteers in particular can provide some added benefit.

It's important to keep in mind, though, that getting a volunteer program off the ground initially requires the investment of a certain amount of time, organization, and planning by the librarian and library worker. What, then, are the rewards? Why bother? First of all, a library exists to serve its community, providing a variety of resources in the form of materials, public computers, classes, events, and other services. In many communities, teens are required by schools or other organizations to take part in community service in order to graduate. Hosting a library teen volunteer program helps meet an educational need that these teens have, much like having database subscriptions helps fill the need for teens to have reliable sources for research, and having tutoring services helps fill the need for teens to study and complete homework successfully.

A teen volunteer program also helps to make the library more visible in the community. Volunteer projects performed by teens can transcend the physical space of the library and give back to the community in very concrete ways: programs aimed at younger children or seniors—for example, a tutoring or Technology Buddy program—are great examples of this. Teen volunteers are excellent partners in marketing library events and can produce promotional materials such as videos for your library. Teen volunteers are also great at word-of-mouth advertising of the library to friends and family members.

Teen volunteers offer many benefits, some of them less expected:

- They can serve as informal focus groups to give you needed feedback. Talk to your teen volunteers regularly about their interests and activities to gain a window into the teen culture of your community.

- Get program ideas from your teen volunteers, or let your volunteers design and lead programs!
- Teen volunteers can also provide needed program support and a core of teen program participants who will attend regularly and bring in other teens.

In addition, volunteering in the library offers workforce development opportunities to teens that they may not be able to get elsewhere in the community. Teen employment hit an all-time low during the height of the recession and has not bounced back completely. As a result, teens across the country are having a hard time finding opportunities to build job-related skills. By providing a teen volunteer program at your library, you're not only getting the help you need; you're also providing a valuable community service to a key segment of the population.

Teen Advisory Boards are a formal way for the library to get regular input from teens, as well as buy-in for library programs. They can help ensure that the overall teen program in the library is meeting the needs of teens in the community, and help you be more effective and efficient by serving as a bellwether—the advisory group can give you key insight during the planning stage to help make sure the program will be of use or interest to the teens. In addition, these boards offer leadership opportunities to teens that they may not be able to get elsewhere in the community.

Never forget that the teens of today are tomorrow's voters and taxpayers. Teens who form a personal relationship with the library by having a positive volunteer experience there are that much more likely to be favorably disposed toward the library when they are adults. Volunteers gain an inside look at the library and all the ways it helps the community—and they will carry this knowledge with them into their adult lives.

DEALING WITH PREEXISTING TEEN VOLUNTEER PROGRAMS AND TEEN ADVISORY BOARDS

Here are the top two pieces of advice for those of you working with a volunteer group or advisory board you didn't design or create yourself:

- Don't feel like you have to change everything.
- Don't feel like you have to keep everything the same.

These guidelines might seem contradictory, but they can be very help-ful. When you first start to examine an existing volunteer program, the key is communication. Talk to the teen members of the program, and ask them about what they like and don't like about it. Ask them why things are the way they are, and what has been working and what hasn't been working. Look at applications, timesheets, handbooks, and other docu-ments, and see if you think there's something missing. Don't feel obli-gated to change everything at once. Don't feel obligated to enact every piece of advice the teens give you. It's less disruptive for the teens, the library, and you to make changes to an established program over time.

You may also find the upcoming suggestions about starting a new teen volunteer program useful, especially if you feel like "business as usual" isn't what you want to do.

STARTING A TEEN VOLUNTEER PROGRAM OR ADVISORY BOARD

Planning

It's important to start with the "why": What need does the library have that a teen volunteer program will fulfill? Once you determine this, then you can begin planning. Your plan doesn't need to be exhaustive or airtight, but it should give you a foundation for making decisions when issues come up, in a way that is in accordance with your library's poli-cies and procedures. Plan on making adjustments and fine-tuning down the road after the program is running for a while. For a quick planning method, take a look at the following checklists. Whether you are start-ing a new teen volunteer group or Teen Advisory Board, or taking on a preexisting program, these checklists will help make sure you have a solid plan.

1. *Volunteer Checklist*
- *Recruitment:* How will you obtain teen volunteers? Will you advertise at the local school, in the newspaper, through the library's website?
- *Schedules:* How do you want volunteers to be scheduled? Will volunteers have set shifts? When will those shifts take place? Will some days be open for unscheduled "drop-ins"?

- *Tracking Hours:* How will volunteer hours be verified? Will volunteers need to sign in and out? Will you have to report hours to anyone, such as Human Resources staff? How will volunteer hours be communicated to the schools? Will volunteer hours be tracked online or on paper? How will volunteers be able to see how many hours they have accumulated?
- *Applications:* Does the library have a volunteer form already? Is it appropriate for teens? Does someone else, such as Human Resources, review incoming volunteer applications? Are background checks required for volunteers, and, if so, would this apply to teen volunteers? Who has final say in what volunteers are accepted? Do you want to interview volunteer candidates or not?
- *Policies:* Is there a volunteer handbook? If so, is it appropriate for teen volunteers? How will volunteers get the handbook? Are you responsible for going over it with them?
- *Supervision:* Who will be in charge of deciding what teen volunteers do and overseeing their work? Should other staff members be able to suggest projects or request assistance from teen volunteers? If so, how? What are volunteers allowed to do, and is there anything that volunteers are not allowed to do per your library policies?
- *Training:* What kind of training should teen volunteers have? Is there a standardized training/orientation process in your library, and, if so, is it teen appropriate? Are there things that all teen volunteers should know: for example, how books are organized in your library?
- *Recognition:* How will the volunteers be celebrated and their work acknowledged? Will there be a "Volunteer of the Month"? An annual pizza party? Some sort of more frequent recognition?

2. Teen Advisory Board Checklist

- *Recruitment:* How will you assemble your advisory group? Will you advertise at the local school, in the newspaper, through the library's website?
- *Meetings:* What day should the group meet, at what time, for how long, and how often?

- *Membership:* Who should be able to join the Teen Advisory Board? Should there be a limit for how many teens can be members of the advisory board at one time? What should the minimum and maximum age for members be? Do you want to stipulate other requirements for membership—for instance, that members must have completed the library summer reading program?
- *Projects:* What do you envision your Teen Advisory Board doing? Leading programs, helping to select materials for the teen section, making posters and displays? What kinds of projects are you comfortable with them doing? What kinds of projects best leverage their interest and expertise?
- *Codes of Conduct:* Are the existing policies and procedures for the library appropriate/adequate for a Teen Advisory Board, or will something additional (but in compliance with the existing policies) need to be created? If so, how will you work with the group to create and disseminate these?
- *Attendance:* Will missing a certain number of meetings mean ejection from the group?
- *Evaluation:* How will you measure whether or not the group is meeting its intended goals and objectives?

For resource to help you put together a teen volunteer program, check out the report from Dosomething.org at https://www.dosomething.org/blog/teens-and-volunteering.

Recruiting

Every librarian and library worker knows that it can be easier to plan a program than to get people to attend it, and teens—often with a variety of curricular and extracurricular activities competing for their interest, or having trouble obtaining transportation to the library—can be a very difficult group to attract. Here are some quick tips for recruiting members for a volunteer program or Teen Advisory Board. Different techniques work better in different communities, and sometimes in the same community at different times. Try a variety of approaches to recruiting and see what works for you.

1. Get into the Schools

One of the easiest ways to recruit volunteers is through the schools, because most teens in your community will attend a public or private school, forming a sort of "captive audience" for your pitch. Many libraries already have a relationship or a network of contacts with local schools, so this may be a relatively easy avenue for recruitment.

- If you visit classrooms already for booktalking, research instruction, or summer reading/learning promotion, bring flyers and talk about your volunteer program.
- If you have contact with teachers, counselors, librarians, or administrators at local high schools and middle schools, share information about your volunteer program with them. They can share the information with teens who need community service hours.
- Try to make your message ubiquitous. Post flyers in the schools if permitted, and get information about your volunteer program into school announcements and newsletters. The more ways that teens are exposed to the library's message, the more likely they are to remember it when the need arises.

2. Market in the Library

You may notice that your library has teen "regulars." Some of them check out books every week, some hang out and do homework, some use the computers, and some appear every summer at the summer reading/learning program. Make sure those teens, who are already positively engaged with the library, know that there is a way to be even more involved.

- Advertise in your library with posters and flyers.
- Advertise in your public computer space, either with physical flyers, or, if possible, with screensavers and other digital reminders.
- Collect e-mail and/or physical addresses of teen summer reading/learning participants (with their permission, of course!), and send invitations to those teens who complete the program. This makes them feel like their work over the summer has unlocked some kind of special achievement, and now they are eligible for something that other people are not.

- Post information on the library's website, Facebook page, or other Internet presence.

3. Capitalize on Word of Mouth

Word of mouth can be especially effective in recruiting teenagers—teens tend to base their choices on recommendations from their friends.[2] Studies of teen information-seeking behavior tend to find friends and family as preferred information sources for teens.[3] But how can you tap into that interpersonal, informal, word-of-mouth marketing?

- If at all possible, don't reject teen volunteer applicants. The more volunteers you have, the more people will be exposed to the idea of volunteering at the library through friends and family members. You can create a snowball effect of volunteering.
- Consider instituting a recruitment bonus for teen volunteers or Teen Advisory Board members who bring in new volunteers or members. This bonus could take the form of a gift card, fine forgiveness coupon, or just a "Volunteer of the Month" certificate, depending on what would work for your library.

4. Reach Out to After-School Programs

Find out where after-school programs are happening in your community, and ask them to help promote the opportunity. Share flyers with them, volunteer to speak at their program, or request that they post information on their website. Use the "Map My Community" tool on the *Find Youth Info* website (www.findyouthinfo.gov/maps/map-my-community). Just put in your zip code to find out what youth-focused programs are being offered in your community.

---

2. The NPD Group, "The NPD Group Reports Teens Credit Word-of-Mouth Most Reliable Shopping Source," August 13, 2012, https://www.npd.com/wps/portal/npd/us/news/press-releases/pr_120813b/.
3. Denise E. Agosto, "People, Places, and Questions: An Investigation of the Everyday Life Information-Seeking Behaviors of Urban Young Adults," *Library and Information Science Research* 27, no. 2 (2008): 141–63, http://www.sciencedirect.com/science/article/pii/S0740818805000046.

GETTING THEM STARTED

Once you have a group of teen volunteers or a Teen Advisory Board, what should they do? How do you convert a group of teens into a force for good in your library? It's a good idea to brainstorm a list of tasks that volunteers can do, and keep this list at the public desk. That way when a volunteer shows up and you've forgotten what you need them to do, you can refer to it. Here are some simple, recurring projects that teen volunteers may be able to help with.

TEEN VOLUNTEER PROJECTS

The key to success is to identify the primary needs of your library and then find a volunteer whose interests and skills can help address that need. You may be surprised at what teens are capable of, so do not limit them to mundane tasks. Doing so makes the experience boring for the teen, who may quit, and it also doesn't help the library achieve its most important work of serving the community. A few examples of work that teen volunteers can do include the following:

1. Design and construct book displays.
2. Assist with or staff the circulation desk to check materials in and out.
3. Lead a storytime for children.
4. Create or maintain a social media presence for the library.
5. Add content to or update your web page.
6. Decorate the library for different seasons and holidays.
7. Design and make promotional materials for library events.
8. Create promotional videos for the library.
9. Test program craft instructions for readability, and make example crafts.
10. Help to supervise the teen space, maybe even staff a small desk. This requires perhaps the most training but makes teen volunteers a very visible part of the library.

11. Help to prepare for children's programs, which often require paper cutting and snack distribution prep work.
12. Write book reviews or create book trailers to encourage other teen patrons to read.
13. Troubleshoot problems with computers or other technical equipment.

THE FIRST TAB MEETING AND TAB MEETING STRUCTURES

Getting a Teen Advisory Board (TAB) started brings its own challenges. A Teen Advisory Board can be viewed as a sort of club, and the teens must get along and work together to get anything done. Here's a sample agenda for your first TAB meeting:

1. Introductions/Icebreakers

Some of your members may know each other already, but it's important to get past the initial cliques. Play a few icebreaker games to help people relax and get to know one another.

ICEBREAKER GAMES

- *Two Truths and a Lie:* Each person tells the group three things about themselves. Two are true, and one isn't. The group has to guess which statement is the lie.
- *Snowball Guess Who:* Participants write little-known facts about themselves on pieces of paper, then crumple them into balls. Everyone throws these "snowballs" around the room for a certain limited amount of time (20–30 seconds works fine), then picks up the ones closest to them, reads them aloud, and tries to guess who wrote them.

- *Group Juggling:* This game requires 4–6 juggling balls, beanbags, or small stuffed animals—and presence of mind. Have participants stand in a circle. Call a person's name and toss the ball to that person. That person will call another's name and toss the ball to them. This process repeats until everyone has caught the ball and thrown it to someone else—no duplicates! Now you've made a pattern, and it always stays the same—each participant always catches the ball from the same person, and throws it to the same person. When the group is confident with the pattern you've made, introduce more and more balls.
- *The Name Dance:* Have participants stand in a circle. Start by saying your first name, and accompanying it with some kind of dance move. The second person has to repeat your name and move, then add their own name and move. Continue until you've reached the last person in the circle, who must attempt to remember everybody's name and dance move.

2. Explain the Vision for the Teen Advisory Board

Make sure participants know what the purpose and mission of the Teen Advisory Board is. Be sure to share your expectations and work with the group to come up with some ground rules. If past members are present, let them share stories of their experiences in the board as well.

3. The Future Direction of the Teen Advisory Board

Now is the time to collect ideas for Teen Advisory Board projects or to have the board vote on ideas you have generated, depending on your personal choice. We find putting up large pieces of paper and letting everyone write their ideas for programs and events on them is a great way to get the ball rolling. After the teens are done writing, talk about each idea, its pros and cons, and see which ideas naturally produce more interest than the others.

4. A Quick, Hands-On Project

It can be helpful to end the first Teen Advisory Board meeting by getting help from the teens to paint a poster or do something else short term and hands-on. This can help them bond as a group and do something beyond planning and discussing, which can bog down TAB meetings. Keep in mind that successful projects are ones that require activities that are hands-on and dynamic. The volunteer programs will not be successful if the majority of the volunteer opportunities are busywork and mundane tasks.

SAMPLE TEEN ADVISORY BOARD PROJECTS

Teen advisory board projects often come out of the members' interests, but here are some ideas to get the ball rolling:

- Evaluate the teen collection, and identify gaps (these could be genres, popular authors, academic topics, etc.).
- Assist with creating a calendar of teen programs for the next several months.
- Prepare a presentation for the library trustees to either celebrate an achievement or make a request for funding or other support.
- Do a visual inventory of the library and brainstorm ways to make it more welcoming to teens.
- Compile a list of youth serving organizations in the community that the librarian or library worker can use for outreach.

MANAGING VOLUNTEERS AND TEEN ADVISORY BOARDS

The idea of managing a group of "unruly" teens might cause you or your staff a little anxiety. With clear expectations and a little preparation, however, managing teens does not need to be frightening for anyone. Take a look at these common pitfalls, and consider how you will address them.

Common Problems and Ways to Address Them

1. Staff Buy-In

As you develop a teen volunteer program or advisory board, it is very important that other staff are involved. You are not omnipresent, and it is crucial that other staff know how to respond to your volunteers when you are not there. Having clear expectations and abundant, easy-to-find information is key to making sure that other staff react to your volunteers with confidence instead of consternation. Here are some ways to make sure others are in the loop on your volunteer program:

- Keep your schedule where other staff can access it, either online or physically. Make sure they know where it is.
- Make sure staff know where your sign-in sheet is, if you have one.
- Make a list of jobs that volunteers can do, and keep it updated. That way, if you are absent, other staff don't have to think of tasks to keep them busy. Ask others for input to this list, as they might occasionally need volunteer assistance for their own projects.
- If you have a teen volunteer handbook, keep it somewhere all staff can find it. Let them know that the volunteers have a code of conduct, and that they can feel confident holding them accountable to it, even when you are not in the vicinity.

2. Absenteeism

Teens can be very reliable volunteers . . . or not. Issues can arise because teens are still learning about personal responsibility, and because they do not have total control over their lives—many rely on others for transportation, and parents, of course, have the right to make decisions or change their mind on issues that can impact a teen's ability to volunteer. As you asked yourself when planning your volunteer program, how will you deal with absences? Will you call your volunteers? Will you expect them to inform you beforehand? Will they be ejected from the program if they build up too many unexcused absences? Make sure your volunteers all know what is expected of them. If you come off as very relaxed about attendance when you orient a volunteer, you can't hold them accountable later down the road if absenteeism becomes a problem with an individual.

Volunteering is a kind of apprenticeship for employment, so promoting attendance is important. Being as strict as an employer would be is probably unnecessary, but consider the following response process:

- Clearly explain your absence policy during volunteer orientation— that you expect them to come on their assigned day and would like a call when they won't be in.
- The first time a volunteer is absent without informing you, remind them of the policy. Let them know why it's important—that people count on them and expect them to be where they say they will be. Ask them if there is a particular issue or challenge they're dealing with that is preventing them from showing up. Ask them to make an action plan to help themselves remember in the future.
- If the volunteer goes several months without another unexpected absence, repeat the above process the next time they are absent. If the volunteer is frequently absent despite reminders, let them know what consequence will occur—whether that's just a note in their file, or rejection from the volunteer program.
- Stick to whatever consequence you decided on.

3. Slacking Off

It's a universal fact that occasionally people just aren't working up to par—whether they need training for a specific skill or a motivational boost. For a teen volunteer, occasional joking with friends or conversing can be a great way to blow off steam. In a Teen Advisory Board, a certain amount of socializing is desirable to cement the group. But if your volunteers are sleeping or web surfing on the job for hours at a time, there is definitely a problem. Occasionally, your teen volunteers may even make things harder for you by not doing their jobs—not cleaning up after a project, for example, can create work and frustration for you or other staff.

- Again, make sure your expectations are clear up front.
- If the issue is training, provide it or find someone who can.
- If the issue is motivation, think of ways to encourage the teen and to make working at the library fun for them and not a chore.

- Ask the teens in question if there are other projects they would rather work on. Genuine engagement is the best way to maintain interest. Consider simply reassigning that teen—if someone regularly fails to clean up after themselves, don't give them creative projects anymore.
- Engage in the disciplinary process detailed in the "Absenteeism" section.

4. Interpersonal Issues

Especially in Teen Advisory Boards, sometimes the natural social divisions and interpersonal differences can create friction among volunteers.

- Focus on building your Teen Advisory Board into a cohesive team at the beginning. Use icebreakers and games to help them get to know one another. If you have a large group, consider doing some kind of exercise at the beginning of each meeting, at least the first few times.
- As much as possible, give equal attention to all Teen Advisory Board members. Be consistent in enforcing your policies to avoid "playing favorites."
- Use caution if splitting your Teen Advisory Board into subcommittees. Make sure the next project recombines the groups to avoid fostering clique behavior.
- Consider distributing a group code of conduct at the beginning of the first meeting to make sure that the whole team has the same norms of behavior, and have them vote to approve it as is, or modify it. Some teens don't mind cursing; others do. Some are unbothered by public displays of affection; others are not. You want to make sure everyone is comfortable in the Teen Advisory Board.

5. Resources for Teen Interns

Not all teen positions in a library have to be unpaid! Resources exist for libraries to provide compensation to teens for the work they do for the library. According to Beth Crist, Youth & Family Services Senior Consultant for Public Libraries in Colorado, "Library Friends groups, foundations, and civic organizations are often the best bet for library grants rather than national grant opportunities, which are both very competitive and usually quite challenging and time-consuming to apply for in these situations." The list below is a recommendation of funding that can be used to pay teen interns at a public library:

- The YALSA/Dollar General Summer Reading Teen Intern Grant will award $1,000 to each of twenty libraries for the purpose of hiring summer teen interns to assist with summer reading activities. Applications are available the January of each year with funds to be used in the next summer: http://summerreading.ning.com/page/summer-reading-grants.

- Many state libraries offer LSTA grants that are broad enough to cover teen interns; there's not one website but library staff can look at their own state library's website for LSTA grants. A list of all state library websites is available at http://www.publiclibraries.com/state_library.htm.

- Local civic organizations—such as the Lions Club, Masons, Junior League, Kiwanis, Rotary, and so on—will often give grants to libraries; library staff can approach their local organizations to ascertain what grants are available and how to apply.

- Starbucks Foundation offers grants for youth leadership (as well as community service); applications are accepted several times throughout each year: http://www.starbucks.com/responsibility/community/starbucks-foundation.

- Many local and state private foundations give grants to libraries and other educational organizations. Library staff can approach their local foundations to ascertain what grants are available and how to apply.

- The Institute of Museum and Library Services (IMLS) offers a range of grants: http://www.imls.gov/applicants/default.aspx.

TEEN VOLUNTEER AND ADVISORY
BOARD ANECDOTES

"We founded a Teen Council group this year for the
first time at my library. Our teen programs are for
ages 11–18. I am thinking about possibly splitting
this group up into two to help with their focus since
this is such a large age range—perhaps into middle
school and high school teens. Right now teens can
apply whenever they are interested—there isn't a set
amount of teens for the group or a deadline for getting in an application. I wanted to make it as open as
possible to start out with and then go from there. The
council meets once a month for 1.5 hours. I save up
questions I have for them about the collection and
programs to ask them, and then we play a game—
we've played some icebreaker-type games as well as
more traditional board games such as Cranium."

—Lauren Knowlton
Teen Services Supervisor
Athens-Clarke County Library, Athens, Georgia

"My words of advice are to let them take the lead as
much as possible. . . . Yes, it's like herding cats or bot-
tling a tornado, but if they feel that they are heard and
that their ideas matter ('Look, I suggested a program
and it happened!'), there will be no stopping you (or
them). There are so many times that they hear no,
it's good to hear yes and feel that they actually have
some power. Even if there is no money, tell them that
and see what creative ways they have to get around
it (potluck parties, bringing stuff from home—you
won't believe all they have to offer)."

"I use volunteers in a multitude of ways, and my TAB is amazing. (It has ranged in size from 3 teens to 80—a banner year a few years ago—and right now I am at about 40 regular attendees.) The only reason any of it works is because they make it work, and I just provide guidance (and a few subtle kicks in the pants when they forget to honor commitments). I also have a leadership group formed from my TAB members who wanted to do more and actually be involved in making programs start to finish rather than just suggesting them."

—Saleena Davidson
South Brunswick Public Library,
South Brunswick, New Jersey

"My TAB has been going strong for five years. I have a group of 10 teens that tend to stay in till they graduate. Every now and then, I will have a few be asked to leave for not pulling their weight, but the teens are the ones who make that decision. They come up with the questions that are on our application each year, and they choose the new members, with me being very much like Vanna White on the whiteboard to help narrow down the candidates and keep everyone on track. We had 27 applicants this year at the Main Library, but we only had 5 openings. Our meeting room only holds 11 comfortably. Our Lock-In combines all three locations of TABs in one location from 9 p.m. till 8 a.m. Nobody sleeps and all the adults there even dress up in costumes for the Murder Mystery. My teens have created programs all on their own with little direction from me, and they put them on

for all ages. The boys two years ago came up with a Football for Dummies program to teach women like myself about football. They figured if they were able to explain it to me where I could understand, then they could do it for others as well. They created a Zombie Survival Program where they went into the history of zombies, they methods of survival if the zombie apocalypse were to happen, and much more. They even created a game to go with this program to see who paid the most attention, and the winner got zombie felties made by me and another staff member for the event. They all do volunteer work with different programs. They will help me out with the craft programs so that I don't have to be in two places at once to assist people; they help other staff members as well with the Spanish computer classes and other events. They volunteer at the bigger events as well such as the author fair, the teen talent show, and several others. As for advice for other librarians and library workers I would say:

- "Let your teens decide how things are going to run. If it is their own, they tend to feel more comfortable keeping it that way and expressing their feelings more often.
- Keep things light at meetings and go with the flow. If you try to push them into talking about something, they won't do it. Adults can be scary or freaky to teens. Mine are all comfortable with talking to me because I still have that teenlike persona about me that lets them open up (I'm 31), and they all say I sound like them. Never talk down to them—talk to them like equals!
- If they go on a tangent while you are trying to talk to them about something totally different, let them ramble for a minute or so and find a way to lead them back to the topic of discussion. In my case, they are so used to

this happening that all I have to do is look at one who isn't afraid to speak up and smile at them, and they help me get things back on track.

- I find that having an agenda at meetings helps a lot and keeps them on track especially if when they are finished with the agenda they then get to play games.

- Let the teens do their homework at meetings. If someone sitting next to them understands something better than they do, then they may just find a study partner (it happens). Also, bring laptops for those who have papers to write, but remember that homework trumps Facebook and make that clear.

- Always have snacks at meetings, even if it's just candy and Capri Sun. If you feed them, they will come.

- Reminders are always helpful. Teens tend to forget things unless they are reminded regularly. I remind mine with e-mails, on Facebook, in person, and sometimes with calls if necessary."

—Hannah Berry
Young Adult Librarian
Aurora Public Library, Aurora, Illinois

"I just had an article published in Tennessee Libraries about my presentation on 'Getting the Most from Your Teen Volunteers' (http://tnla.org/displaycommon.cfm?an=1&subarticlenbr=553) and more info on my webpage: www.tinyurl.com/BethDKenneth."

—Beth D. Kenneth
Teen Librarian
Memphis Public Library, Memphis, Tennessee

"I have a really great TAB group that I've been running for about a year now. I've changed a couple things since I started out to make everything run more smoothly. The most important thing I've started doing is creating an official agenda and making copies for everyone. They get off task so easily, and it really helps to have a list of things to keep bringing them back to. For my group, I've also found that when it comes to making decisions about things (like program ideas or display ideas), it works best to give them a limited number of options rather than to keep things open-ended. I'll ask, 'Should we do x, y, or z for our Halloween program?' rather than 'What should we do for Halloween?' as it keeps them from getting overwhelmed or going overboard with difficult to execute or expensive ideas."

—Jessica Hilburn
Teen Services and Reference Librarian
Newburyport Public Library,
Newburyport, Massachusetts

ADDITIONAL RESOURCES

- YALSA archived webinars (accessible at www.ala.org/yalsa/webinars):
  ○ "A TAG Can Work for You, Too!" (2012)

WORKS CITED

Agosto, Denise E. "People, Places, and Questions: An Investigation of the Everyday Life Information-Seeking Behaviors of Urban Young Adults." *Library and Information Science Research* 27, no. 2 (2008): 141–63. http://www.sciencedirect.com/science/article/pii/S0740818805000046.

Bureau of Labor Statistics. "Volunteering in the United States, 2012." United States Department of Labor. February 22, 2013. http://www. bls.gov/news.release/archives/volun_02222013.pdf.

NPD Group, "The NPD Group Reports Teens Credit Word-of-Mouth Most Reliable Shopping Source." August 13, 2012. https://www.npd. com/wps/portal/npd/us/news/press-releases/pr_120813b/.

7 | Providing Virtual Library Services to Help Teens (& you) 24/7

TODAY'S TEENS ARE often referred to as "digital natives,"[1] young people who have grown up with the Internet, mobile devices, and social networks as facts of life. According to the Pew Internet and American Life Project, 95% of teens go online, 80% own a computer, 37% own a smartphone, and 23% own a tablet. A digital divide still exists, however: computer and tablet ownership is lower among low-income teens, African American teens, and Hispanic teens.[2] A library has a balancing act to do: library workers can't assume that every teen is connected with an iPod or a cell phone, but we can't ignore social media and mobile platforms either. Technology trends seem to change faster and faster all the time, but this chapter will give some general tips and advice for diving in or just dipping your toes in social networks and mobile technology. It will explore many ways that librarians and library workers can use technology to reach and serve teens, including the following:

- Guide to using social media platform to interact with teen patrons.
- How to get started with social media—even if you've never run a social media page before.
- Guide for integrating mobile technology into your library.

---

1. Marc Prensky, "Digital Natives, Digital Immigrants," *On the Horizon* 9, no. 5 (October 2001), http://www.marcprensky.com/writing/Prensky%20-%20Digital%20Natives,%20 Digital%20Immigrants%20-%20Part1.pdf.
2. Joanna Brenner, "Pew Internet: Teens," *Pew Internet and American Life Project*, May 21, 2012, http://pewinternet.org/Commentary/2012/April/Pew-Internet-Teens.aspx.

According to the YALSA report *The Future of Library Services for and with Teens: A Call to Action,* creating virtual spaces allows teens to connect with other teens who share similar interests and to interact with experts, coaches, and mentors who can help teens not only build digital-literacy skills, but expand their learning beyond the school day based on their interests. Likewise, with the diverse populations in the United States, technology access is not a universal opportunity because "ownership of technology devices continues to vary across socioeconomic and racial demographics."[3] Libraries act as a bridge, allowing equal access to these important technological components, and they are the place where teens can learn the skills that will help prepare them for a successful career in the future.

Libraries are the essential nexus for delivering services and disseminating information through online or mobile technologies. Libraries may help teens build digital-literacy skills that they will need in order to learn how to use online and mobile resources ethically. Likewise, teens must incorporate technology into their future careers in order to be competitive in the current job market. Teen services that utilize online/mobile technologies are able to extend the reach of their teen services program—even libraries with a small staff can easily use online resources to amplify their face-to-face efforts in serving teens. Be sure to check out YALSA's "Teen Space Guidelines" (http://www.ala.org/yalsa/guidelines/teenspaces), as there is a section in that document that addresses best practices in creating and maintaining virtual spaces for and with teens.

Before you spend precious time and resources building out a web or mobile presence for the teens in your community, determine what your primary goal is. Is it to provide 24/7 homework assistance? To connect teens with coaches and mentors who can help them explore careers? Is it to raise awareness about the value that the library provides to the community? Or is it simply to market library events and programs? As always, answering this question goes back to knowing what the most pressing needs are of the teens in your community. Once you know the

---

3. Linda W. Braun, Maureen L. Hartman, Sandra Hughes-Hassell, and Kafi Kumasi, with contributions from Beth Yoke, *The Future of Library Services for and with Teens: A Call to Action,* January 8, 2014, http://www.ala.org/yaforum/sites/ala.org.yaforum/files/content/YALSA_nationalforum_final.pdf.

purpose for creating or enhancing your online presence, then you will be able to decide which type of online tools are the best fit for your needs.

SOCIAL MEDIA

Social media has changed the way people interact and represent themselves online in a fundamental way, and many organizations have capitalized on social networks to connect people and share information. The majority of teens who are online (81%) have some kind of social media connection. Of teens who are on social media, 94% had Facebook accounts in 2012 and 26% had Twitter accounts.[4] Social media platforms, however, can wax and wane in popularity: remember when MySpace was popular? If you are getting involved in social media for your library, be flexible—your audience will migrate between platforms as new generations of teens grow up and new tools are developed. Any guide to individual social media platforms might be obsolete in a few years, so, instead, here is a guide to getting involved in any social media environment.

1. Start with Research

Where are online are the teens in your community? Facebook? Twitter? Instagram? Take polls (offer incentives if necessary), start discussions, and look at research. The Pew Internet and American Life Project is a great resource for data on social media, mobile technology, and Internet use among teens.

2. Think about Policy

Does your library have a social media policy or another policy that governs its online communication and presence? If so, make yourself familiar with it before you create any official library accounts. If not, you may want to consider writing one yourself. The on-demand webinar "Tweet, Link, Like: Creating a Social Media Policy for Your Library"[5] may be helpful to you. Talk to members of your community relations

---

4. Brenner, "Pew Internet: Teens."
5. This webinar is available from YALSA, "Tweet, Link, Like: Creating a Social Media Policy for Your Library," *Webinars on Demand*, American Library Association, 2011, http://www.ala.org/yalsa/onlinelearning/webinars/webinarsondemand.

department or administrators about the issues surrounding an organizational social media account, because you will probably need their stamp of approval before you can go live. When thinking about a social media policy, consider the following questions:

- Who is allowed to make posts?
- Who is allowed to post comments?
- What kinds of comments can be or should be deleted?
- What kinds of posts are appropriate and what kinds of posts are not?
- Are there copyright concerns that could apply to some content?
- Are there patron privacy concerns that apply to some content, such as photos of patrons or works created by patrons?

3. Think about Content

What would you want to share through the organizational account? Would it be primarily a way to advertise library programs? Would you solicit feedback from patrons? Would you post photos? Would you post content generated by teens? Social media experts recommend using a social media account not simply as an advertising mechanism, but as a way to engage with your customers. Commercial Facebook pages do this by offering incentives, posting content that others want to share, and asking questions.[6] Look at other libraries' social media accounts, or even some brands' social media accounts, and see which ones are the most interesting and successful.

Another important point to consider is your audience. Would this platform be designed purely for teens, or would adult library patrons also interact with it? Would this change what kinds of things you post?

4. Make a Trial Page

Before your page goes live, make a mock-up trial account to show your administrators what it would look like. Set up a hidden or personal

---

6. Mari Smith, "Five Ways to Increase Your Facebook Engagement," *Social Media Examiner*, September 10, 2012, http://www.socialmediaexaminer.com/facebook-engagement/.

account and create sample posts of the kind of things you think would interest teens: photos, teen-created works, announcements, and so on. If appropriate for your library, ask your teen volunteers to post sample comments or content on this trial page to create a more accurate representation of your final product.

5. Consider Curation

Think about how the page will be maintained and by whom. Being the only person in charge of a social media platform can be exhausting and lead to infrequent postings. Consistent, frequent updates are important to maintaining a healthy online presence. Think about how often you want the page to be updated. If you are working with someone else, make sure you try to avoid double posts.

MOBILE TECHNOLOGY

More and more people, especially teens, engage with the world through mobile technologies like phones and tablets. According to the Pew Internet and American Life Project, 78% of teens have a cell phone, 37% of all teens own smartphones (up from 23% in 2011), 74% of teens access the Internet on mobile devices, and one in four use the Internet primarily on their phones as opposed to laptops or PCs.[7] Low-income teens are even more likely than others to access the Internet through mobile devices.[8] Despite this fact, many libraries are not yet engaging with mobile platforms at all. According to the "ALA Library Fact Sheet 6," only 15% of public library websites are optimized for mobile use.[9] In a fundamental way, these libraries have no presence in the virtual space that teens primarily inhabit. According to YALSA's *Future of Library*

7. Kristen Purcell, "10 Things to Know about How Teens Use Technology," *Pew Internet and American Life Project*, July 10, 2013, http://www.pewinternet.org/Presentations/2013/Jul/10-Things-to-Know-About-HowTeens-Use-Technology.aspx.
8. Mary Madden et al. "Teens and Technology 2013," *Pew Internet and American Life Project*, March 13, 2013, http://www.pewinternet.org/Reports/2013/Teens-and-Tech.aspx.
9. American Library Association, "Public Library Use: ALA Library Fact Sheet 6," June 2013, http://www.ala.org/tools/libfactsheets/alalibraryfactsheet06.

Services for and with Teens, "There are over 40 million adolescents, aged 12–17, living in the United States today, and they use libraries. A 2013 Pew survey found that 72% of 16- to 17-year-olds had used a public library in 2012."[10]

Many libraries do not yet have the capacity to build mobile apps or overhaul their entire site to make it fully compatible with mobile devices, so here are some ways to become more mobile-friendly:

1. Integrate Technology into Programs

What unusual, interesting, or underappreciated resources are hiding out in your library? Could you utilize Instagram or Facebook to create an online group for teens to engage in library programming? Ask your Teen Advisory Board what they would like to experience. Consult the *YALSAblog* and reach out to other members for programming ideas (http://yalsa.ala.org/blog/). Could other community organizations be involved? For example, organize a community-wide mobile scavenger hunt, using SCVNGR.[11]

2. Recommend and Use Apps

Many fun, educational mobile apps are also free or low cost. Consider sharing the *YALSAblog*'s "App of the Week" recommendation with your teen patrons and posting a link to it on your library web page or social media page. For other places to find apps, check out the American Association of School Libraries' new list of "Best Apps for Teaching and Learning"[12] and the *School Library Journal*'s app reviews.[13] Teen patrons can also be helpful for finding apps. Consider hosting "Bring Your Own Device" programs to teach teens how to use some of these free apps to create movies, make 3D models, or design their own games. YALSA's

---

10. Braun et al., *Future of Library Services for and with Teens*.
11. *SCVNGR*, http://www.scvngr.com/builder.
12. American Association of School Librarians, "Best Apps for Teaching and Learning," American Library Association, 2014, http://www.ala.org/aasl/standards-guidelines/best-apps.
13. "Archives for Reviews/Apps," *School Library Journal*, 2014, http://www.slj.com/category/books-media/reviews/apps/.

free Teen Book Finder app is a great resource to help library staff with readers' advisory and collection development.

3. Host a Device Petting Zoo

Many libraries have begun loaning out devices such as iPads. If your library does this, consider talking to your administration about pre-loading these devices with teen-friendly apps and making them available to teens. Connecting with a local store, such as Best Buy, can be a great way to implement this program. They may be willing not only to lend the devices, but also provide volunteers who can demonstrate how to use them. Here are some specific questions to consider if you want to implement device lending for teens:

- Will you have a device-use agreement/contract? Fines for a lost or damaged device can be hefty, even for adults. Make sure teens comprehend this.
- Will teens need parental consent to borrow devices?
- Will teens be allowed to take the devices out of the library, or will they have to use them in-house?
- What will be the minimum age of a patron who can borrow a device?

TEEN WEB PAGES

Why have a teen page on your library website?[14] Many of the same reasons for having a physical space for teens apply to virtual spaces as well. It's also critical to realize that your library's hours are limited and the library may be closed during times when teens need it the most: on evenings and weekends. A library's teen page is available 24/7 and can be a key resource in helping teens with school projects. It can also be a place where books and other materials are featured, where topics of interests to teens can be explored, and where teens can potentially share

---

14. YALSA, "Teen Space Guidelines," American Library Association. 2011–12, http://www.ala.org/yalsa/guidelines/teenspaces.

content of their own. When thinking about the development of the teen web page, consider these questions:

- Will you have a page on the library's website or a separate website or blog all your own?
- If your teen page is on the library website, can it include blog-style content that changes and updates regularly—book reviews, technology how-to's, library news, and so on?
- Is there a way to integrate interactive features such as polls?
- Is there a place for teens to submit questions for a library worker and perhaps see others' questions?
- Can you integrate a Twitter feed or other social media content?
- Is there a way to have live reference help—chat reference, for example—built into the page?

Whatever platform you are using to host your teen library page, consider the following general topics:

1. What Do Teens Need to Know?

This can include not only library information such as hours and contact info, but also links to homework help, test-prep sites, library databases, and college application and financial aid information. Information and how-to's on technology and online privacy could also be very valuable, as could the contact information for social services in the area.

2. What Would Teens Like to Know?

Fun, recreational information falls under this category. Book, film, game and music reviews, links to cool DIY crafts, library videos, recommended websites, and information on recreational library programs and other community events can all have a home on your teen web page.

3. How Can Your Site Foster Interaction, Communication, and Conversation?

Information on the Internet isn't a one-way street anymore—users expect to be able to communicate, connect, and contribute. Think about your website as a potential avenue for virtual "passive programs." Can you have a virtual book club via a forum or comment thread? Can you have a caption or meme contest? Perhaps even ask obscure literary trivia questions for the chance to win a free book? Consider the workload and responsibilities that this extra avenue of communication will bring to you and your coworkers. Questions should be responded to promptly, or patrons will become frustrated. Is there one staff member who can be responsible for checking questions daily? Is it a task of whoever is staffing the public services desk at opening or closing? Is it the responsibility of many people?

Whether you work with an IT department, web designer, or a volunteer to develop your teen web page or you create your own teen blog using a WordPress or Blogger account, think of making the teen page visually similar to the library page, but with its own unique branding in colors, logos, or images. Make sure the appearance of your page isn't dated or visually confusing. Run your ideas and designs by some other people including actual teenagers. The graphic design, communications, or information technology department at your local college or university may be a good place to look for pro bono help.

EXAMPLES OF GOOD TEEN LIBRARY WEBSITES

- http://teens.librarypoint.org/: Includes book suggestions, technology advice, and book recommendations.
- http://tatalonline.blogspot.com/: Good example of a blog used as a teen page.
- http://tscpl.org/blog/teen/: A teen blog that integrates well with the library page.

TEEN-CREATED CONTENT

Whatever form your teen web page takes, consider taking advantage of the ability to incorporate teen-created content. A library website can give teen authors and artists the chance to have their work recognized and even "published" for the appreciation of others. Not only is this great validation for teens—it can also help a teen stand out when applying for jobs, internships, and colleges. Here are some steps to consider when working with teen-generated content:

1. Who Is Allowed to Contribute?

Are there age limits to who can submit content for your page? If your district has a consistent age that they consider as "teen," will it match the submission-age limit or not? Can anyone submit content or only members of certain groups—writing clubs or Teen Advisory Boards?

2. Who Vets Content?

Who is the person in charge of deciding what gets posted? Is it you? Other staff members? A panel of teens? One teen? You may consider writing up content guidelines and policies to make sure selection is fair and unbiased—consider writing these guidelines with the input of your teens.

3. What Kind of Content Do You Want?

Are there any limits on what kinds of things you will post? Will you accept art, videos, audio, or only writing? Are there certain things that would make a piece unacceptable for posting? For example, will works containing profanity, violence, or nudity be prohibited? If teens are helping you manage content, bring up these questions and consider their responses. Also, consider rules and regulations governing original content. Will there be any procedure to check if a submitted work has been plagiarized? Who will have that responsibility? If a video is an original work but contains copyrighted music or film clips, will that be a problem? Since patrons' original works will be posted online, look into some licensing method for them, such as Creative Commons licenses, an alternative to copyright that is more customizable and easy to embed in a website.[15]

4. How Will You Get the Ball Rolling and Keep It Rolling?

Consider getting a group of teens to be your seed posters, and start the blog or web page off with consistent content updates. Think about how

---

15. *Creative Commons*, http://creativecommons.org/.

to encourage posts and submissions—contests might be a good way to spark interest, as well as getting in touch with creative-writing teachers, school newspapers, and literary magazines. Again, think about collecting ideas from teens for contests and promotions.

5. How Will You Protect Teen Privacy?
Although teen posters will probably benefit from their work gaining exposure, online privacy is an important concern, especially for minors. Consider what you will do to make sure that teen contributors' work is acknowledged but that their identities are still protected.

10 QUICK CONTENT PROMPTS

1. Six-Word Memoirs
2. Zombie Haiku
3. Who can make the best BookFace[16] self-portrait using a book cover?
4. Video reviews of teens' favorite books
5. Redesign a book cover—either to make it better, or to make it hilariously worse.
6. Book Spine Poetry
7. Tell a classic literary plot via tweets, texts, or Facebook posts, à la Twitterature.[17]
8. Make a book trailer.
9. Make an original audio drama, or turn a scene from your favorite book into an audio drama.
10. Make a modern vlog version of your favorite book, à la *The Lizzie Bennet Diaries*.[18]

16. *Sleeveface*, http://www.sleeveface.com/.
17. Alexander Aciman and Emmett Rensin, *Twitterature* (New York: Penguin, 2009).
18. "The Lizzie Bennet Diaries," *YouTube*, http://www.youtube.com/user/LizzieBennet.

KEEPING UP-TO-DATE

As we all know, technology changes rapidly in unpredictable ways, and it's easy to get out-of-date. Technology awareness is not a psychic ability, but a habit that can be cultivated. Subscribe to blogs, check in with tech websites, ask questions, and attend conferences, and soon you will be the one people ask about new developments. Here are some good resources to start with:

1. Online Classes

If you want to dig deep and learn a lot more about technology on your own time, these resources may be right for you:

- *http://www.codecademy.com/: Codecademy* uses interactive mini-lessons to teach computer programming, including HTML, CSS, Java, Python, PHP, and more. Best of all, it's free!
- *http://www.alatechsource.org/workshops: ALA TechSource* offers small-group workshops on library-specific topics, led by experts, and designed with hands-on learning in mind. These workshops are not free, but your employer may have a training budget to cover them.
- *https://www.edx.org/course-list/allschools/allsubjects/allcourses:* If you want to study in-depth, an edX course in computer science might be the way to go. EdX courses come out of universities like Harvard, MIT, and Berkeley, but take place 100% online. Courses themselves are free, but some may require textbooks.

2. Tech Blogs and Websites

These sites are worth subscribing to if you want to keep abreast of the world of tech:

- http://www.pewinternet.org/: The Pew Internet and American Life Project is the all-time best site for research on how Americans interact with the Internet and mobile technology.
- http://mashable.com/: *Mashable* collects the latest in news on tech and social media—as well other trends. Worth keeping up with, but beware of getting lost in it for an entire morning.

- *http://www.socialmediaexaminer.com/: Social Media Examiner* contains advice on using social media for businesses that is very applicable to libraries, plus shows examples of good corporate social media pages.
- *http://news.cnet.com/: CNET News* collects interesting technology news daily from all over the world.

3. Library-Specific Resources

These websites focus specifically on how technology affects libraries:

- *http://www.americanlibrariesmagazine.org/alnews: American Libraries* magazine's online platform covers more subjects than just technology and is worth a regular check-in, even if you subscribe to the print version.
- *http://oedb.org/blog/:* The *iLibrarian Blog* is a collection of interesting news and useful tutorials for the tech-curious librarian.
- *http://www.techsoupforlibraries.org/blog: Tech Soup for Libraries* includes case studies, articles, and occasionally webinars all about technology in libraries.

When you think of diving into technology, be brave. You don't have to do everything at once—start with something that you are comfortable with and move up from there. Many tools, classes, and resources exist to help you begin and gain skills. Tap into experts in your own community who can help you. The key is getting started.

ADDITIONAL RESOURCES

- YALSA archived webinars (accessible at www.ala.org/yalsa/webinars):
  o "Apps, Apps, Everywhere" (2013)
  o "I'm Tweeting on the Inside" (2013)

WORKS CITED

"Archives for Reviews/Apps," *School Library Journal*. 2014. http://www.slj.com/category/books-media/reviews/apps/.

Aciman, Alexander, and Emmett Rensin. *Twitterature*. New York: Penguin, 2009.

American Association of School Librarians. "Best Apps for Teaching and Learning." American Library Association. 2014. http://www.ala.org/aasl/standards-guidelines/best-apps.

American Library Association. "Public Library Use: ALA Library Fact Sheet 6." June 2013. http://www.ala.org/tools/libfactsheets/alalibraryfactsheet06.

Braun, Linda W. Maureen L. Hartman, Sandra Hughes-Hassell, and Kafi Kumasi, with contributions from Beth Yoke. *The Future of Library Services for and with Teens: A Call to Action*. January 8, 2014. http://www.ala.org/yaforum/sites/ala.org.yaforum/files/content/YALSA_nationalforum_final.pdf.

Brenner, Joanna. "Pew Internet: Teens." *Pew Internet and American Life Project*. May 21, 2012. http://pewinternet.org/Commentary/2012/April/Pew-Internet-Teens.aspx.

Creative Commons. http://creativecommons.org/.

"The Lizzie Bennet Diaries." *YouTube*. http://www.youtube.com/user/LizzieBennet.

Madden, Mary, et al. "Teens and Technology 2013." *Pew Internet and American Life Project*. March 13, 2013. http://www.pewinternet.org/Reports/2013/Teens-and-Tech.aspx.

Prensky, Marc. "Digital Natives, Digital Immigrants." *On the Horizon* 9, no. 5 (October 2001). http://www.marcprensky.com/writing/Prensky%20-%20Digital%20Natives,%20Digital%20Immigrants%20-%20Part1.pdf.

Purcell, Kristen. "10 Things to Know about How Teens Use Technology." *Pew Internet and American Life Project*. July 10, 2013. http://www.pewinternet.org/Presentations/2013/Jul/10-Things-to-Know-About-HowTeens-Use-Technology.aspx.

SCVNGR. http://www.scvngr.com/builder.

Sleeveface. http://www.sleeveface.com/.

Smith, Mari. "Five Ways to Increase Your Facebook Engagement." *Social Media Examiner*. September 10, 2012. http://www.socialmediaexaminer.com/facebook-engagement/.

YALSA. "Teen Space Guidelines." American Library Association. 2011–12. http://www.ala.org/yalsa/guidelines/teenspaces.

YALSA. "Tweet, Link, Like: Creating a Social Media Policy for Your Library." *Webinars on Demand*. American Library Association. 2011. http://www.ala.org/yalsa/onlinelearning/webinars/webinarsondemand.

8 | Increasing your Impact with Community Partnerships

LET'S FACE IT: the needs of your community are great, and you cannot solve them on your own. Partnerships bring together different organizations to solve a problem, and the good news is that there are lots of individuals and organizations in your community who care about youth. Forming partnerships with these groups can increase program effectiveness, program relevance, political leverage, visibility, reputation, organizational capacity, and revenue streams. Establishing a partnership will likely take up a lot of your time initially, but the benefits are well worth it. This chapter covers the following:

- Real-life examples of successful community partnerships.
- How to create and maintain fruitful partnerships.
- A guide to managing projects with partners.

According to the YALSA report *The Future of Library Services for and with Teens: A Call to Action*, of the "40 million adolescents, aged 12–17, living in the United States today . . . a 2013 Pew survey found that 72% of 16- to 17-year-olds had used a public library in 2012."[1] These teens can benefit from a networked public library that creates opportunities for their patrons. Developing community partnerships at

---

1. Linda W. Braun, Maureen L. Hartman, Sandra Hughes-Hassell, and Kafi Kumasi, with contributions from Beth Yoke, *The Future of Library Services for and with Teens: A Call to Action*, January 8, 2014, http://www.ala.org/yaforum/sites/ala.org.yaforum/files/content/YALSA_nationalforum_final.pdf.

the public library begins with identifying what the needs are of the teens in the community, then seeking out those organizations, agencies, and businesses that have the resources to help meet those needs.

Libraries are community hubs, bringing people and organizations together in a common, safe space. One way libraries serve this function in their community is by actively seeking and cultivating partnerships with other organizations. Community partnerships can enhance library services for and with teens in a variety of ways:

- Helping you achieve more than you could by yourself.
- Expanding the library's audience by tapping into the networks of other organizations—which may include teens who have never visited the library.
- Saving resources by giving the library access to those it does not already have, or by sharing the cost of purchasing new resources.
- Increasing the library's visibility and relevance in the community at large, which can be an important factor when library funding comes up for votes.

At this point, you may be wondering how to begin a partnership, especially if you have never tried anything like it before. This chapter will provide a quick guide to seeking out and partnering with other organizations.

COLLECTIVE IMPACT

Collective impact is the commitment of entities from different sectors in the community to a common agenda for solving a specific social problem. The idea of collective impact was first shared in the *Stanford Social Innovation Review*'s 2011 article "Collective Impact,"[2] written by John Kania, managing director at the consulting firm FSG, and Mark Kramer, Kennedy School at Harvard and cofounder of FSG. The concept

---

2. John Kania and Mark Kramer, "Collective Impact," *Stanford Social Innovation Review* 9, no. 1 (Winter 2011), http://www.ssireview.org/articles/entry/collective_impact.

of collective impact hinges on the idea that in order for organizations to create lasting solutions to social problems on a large scale, they need to coordinate their efforts and work together around a clearly defined goal. This approach can be new for many libraries, who in the past may have primarily worked alone to address community needs. Collective impact discourages this type of isolation, pointing out that communities benefit most when organizations create cross-sector coalitions to make meaningful and sustainable progress on key social issues, such as high dropout rates in high schools. This approach toward solving community problems has been recognized by the White House Council for Community Solutions as an important framework for progress on social issues, and it is well worth it for libraries to explore this option in their own communities. The Collective Impact Forum can be a good starting place for learning more about this approach to addressing community needs and determining how your library might benefit from embracing it (http://collectiveimpactforum.org/). Another resource that provides practical resources for libraries is the Community Tool Box (http://ctb.ku.edu/en).

Related to collective impact is community development, which is a process where members of a community come together to take collective action and find solutions to common problems at the local level. It's a broad term encompassing the actions of civic leaders, activists, involved citizens, and others to improve various aspects of communities. The goal of community development is to empower both individuals and groups by providing them with the skills they need to effect change within their own communities. These skills are often created through the formation of large social groups whose purpose is to take collective action around a common agenda. Increasingly, community development is a topic of interest to local decision makers and elected officials, so it is important for libraries to be aware of this movement and to make sure that libraries are included in discussions related to community development. To learn more about it, check out a collection of essays and articles on the topic: *Investing in What Works for America's Communities: Essays on People, Place and Purpose*, which can be found at http://www.whatworksforamerica.org/.

Libraries that embrace the principles behind collective impact and contribute to community development activities in their towns will position themselves as an indispensable community resource that is actively engaged in helping to solve local issues. Creating partnerships is a first step toward a collective impact approach.

STARTING A PARTNERSHIP

Begin with a Need

What is it that teens in your community need the most? Job-skills training? Access to twenty-first-century technology? Help with transitioning from high school to adulthood? YALSA's *The Future of Library Services for and with Teens* cites the need for libraries to "bridge the growing digital and knowledge divide: School and public libraries must ensure that in addition to providing access to digital tools, that they also provide formal and informal opportunities for teens to learn to use them in meaningful and authentic ways."[3] Local community college or high school librarians may be great resources for technology workshops or hands-on training if your library wants to offer digital-literacy or technology-skills training.

According to Judy Zuckerman, Director of Youth and Family Services at Brooklyn Public Library, partnerships with libraries involve creative thinking and working with businesses in the community. "Besides contacting schools, librarians and library workers may attend community meetings and try to speak to raise awareness about the library . . . [also] if the library has great program spaces and can guarantee an audience many community agencies here [in Brooklyn] initiate the contact and come to us."

Whether the need is large or small, give it some serious thought. What do you want to accomplish? What role would your community partner play in this project? What do you expect to gain and what can your partner gain? Prepare an "elevator speech" to explain your idea for addressing

---

3. Braun et al., *Future of Library Services.*

the need. A good elevator speech should explain your idea concisely and convincingly in just a few sentences. With a good idea and a good pitch, you can start looking for partners. When crafting your pitch, make sure it answers the following questions:

- What do you want to do?
- So what? Why is it important?
- What's in it for the person you are talking to?

Inventory Your Assets

Whether you realize it or not, libraries have a lot to bring to a partnership:

- Meeting and display spaces
- A newsletter, website, and social media presence
- Highly trained staff
- Direct access to community members
- A network of existing community groups, partners, supporters, and volunteers
- The capacity to implement programs
- A wealth of in-depth, quality information, tools, and resources
- A focus on serving the entire community
- Volunteer opportunities
- Good PR/reputation enhancement
- Donation/sponsorship opportunities

Be prepared to articulate these assets when you approach potential partners, so they can understand what you can contribute to a collaborative project.

Identify and Vet Potential Partners

Think of a partnership as dating—it has to be a good match for both parties. You'll want to do some research to find an organization that meets your needs and is closely aligned with your goals. When looking for partners, you might consider these strategies:

- *Mine your library:* Your colleagues and the library volunteers have connections that you do not, connections you may not even have considered.
- *Mine your own circles:* You are a part of your community. Think of the friends and acquaintances you have, what businesses you frequent, what clubs you belong to, and so on. You might have connections you haven't considered.
- *Do some cold-calling:* Explore social networks to find contact information for potentially relevant groups. Go out and contact local businesses who are relevant to your idea. Call teachers and other school officials. Make sure your elevator speech is at the ready!
- Do research to find out which of these are in your community:
  - After-School All-Stars
  - After-school programs (can be at schools, community centers, religious organizations, and neighborhood associations)
  - Boys and Girls Clubs of America
  - Boy Scouts and Girl Scouts
  - Campfire USA
  - 4-H Clubs
  - Girls, Inc.
  - Immigrant organizations
  - Museums
  - Parks and Recreation Departments
  - Police Athletic Leagues
  - Religious organizations
  - Social service agencies
  - Youth-focused organizations and nonprofits

To help your research, use the "Map My Community" tool the *Find Youth Info* website (www.findyouthinfo.gov/maps/map-my-community).

An important part of seeking community partners may be to change the way you see the world. According to researcher Richard Wiseman, people who consider themselves "lucky" tend to be more open to the world around them and notice opportunities where others do not.[4] In one experiment, Wiseman had subjects count the number of photos in a newspaper. People who described themselves as "lucky" were more likely to notice an ad on page two saying: "Stop Counting—There are 43 Photographs in This Newspaper." I would never say that careful planning and preparation are not important, but a key part of nurturing community partnerships is to cultivate "luck" or to make yourself open to chance partnerships. Start to look at the world around you with library-vision. When you talk to people, mention your projects and see what sparks. Listen to patrons and friends when they talk about their hobbies. Notice which businesses are closing and opening around town. Get out more. Try new things. Your community is full of opportunities for partnerships that are waiting to be tapped. Agencies that are good partners depend on what you want them as partners for and what they can provide. Local businesses are great partners: they donate prizes, provide program leaders, and advertise programs to their clientele. "Fan" groups are great partners, too—often they'd love to help plan events for their fandom, and the library can give them a venue for their activities. After-school groups are also great: a library can provide Programs-in-a-Box to middle school after-school groups. The library gets a bigger audience, and the school gets free activities for the kids.

In the process of developing and seeking partnerships, you may need to train yourself to say yes rather than no. Occasionally, opportunities will present themselves to you when other organizations approach the library with ideas for partnerships. In this situation, it can be easy to say no—everyone is busy after all, and you have your own programs to plan. Saying yes to other groups also carries an element of risk at times. The other organization might be a bit of an unknown quantity, or you may simply feel comfortable with your own schedule of events and not want to add anything to the mix. If someone comes to you with a partnership idea, try to give them a fair hearing before simply saying no or assuming it won't work in your library.

---

4. Michael Shermer, "As Luck Would Have It," *Scientific American*, March 26, 2006, http://www.scientificamerican.com/article.cfm?id=as-luck-would-have-it.

Finally, while seeking community partnerships, remember that the onus rests on you to make things happen. If forming a community partnership matters to you, be persistent in pursuing it. Don't give up if one group doesn't get back to you—try a different group, a different person within the same group, or a different pitch.

Building and Maintaining Partnerships

Once you have identified a partner and your organizations have agreed to work together, a key first step is to create a Memorandum of Understanding. This formal document lays out exactly what each party will do. Working together to create this at the start of the partnership is a proactive step that can eliminate problems later. When you have a group of people gathered around to work toward a common goal, you will have to bring them together to plan and work. This is where the real labor of creating the project happens, and in this situation your partnership will live or die based on how well you communicate with your partners. Face-to-face meetings don't have to be the only way for you and your partners to keep in touch: video chat, e-mail, or collaborative documents stored on a system like Google Drive might work better for your group. For some smaller partnerships, face-to-face meetings may be completely unnecessary. In any case, make sure everyone knows the important things:

- What their jobs are in the partnership.
- What the project deadlines are.
- What emergent issues or roadblocks have come up recently.
- How to get in touch with you and other members of the group, and how frequently they should be getting in touch with you.
- How the project is progressing from stage to stage.

Err on the side of over-communicating as opposed to under-communicating. In a collaborative project, it is far more likely that you have not said enough than that you have said too much. People may need to be reminded of important information more than you might expect. Don't make people try to read your mind. It is very important that all members of a collaborative project know where they stand, what is expected of them, and when any deliverables are needed. Remind, update, and remind again to make sure everyone is on the same page.

It is also important to keep in mind that different organizations have different cultures. Businesses and nonprofits, including libraries, also have differing organizational capacities, motivations, and purposes. Nonprofits such as libraries are driven by their social missions to generate positive community returns. Businesses are driven by the need to generate profits and increase value for shareholders. Different cultures can impact communication. It's important to develop a shared language. For example, what does "This has to happen now" mean to your library? Does it mean today, this week, this month, or this year? Does your partner share that same definition? Knowing about the culture and language of your partner is a key to facilitating good communication.

THE FIRST MEETING: A SAMPLE AGENDA

1. Introductions and icebreaker activity
2. Discussion of the issue and goals of the partnership
   o What is the project?
   o What are the big goals of this project?
   o What is the project timeline?

3. Generate ideas
   o How can we reach those goals?
   o Who can contribute what skills and resources?

4. Allocate tasks
   o What should be done by the next meeting, and by whom?

5. Set communication protocols
   o How will you keep in touch and how frequently?

6. Set next meeting

Implementation

Once you and your partner(s) agree to a collaboration, the next step is to co-develop a program that addresses the needs of the teens in the community. Key activities during this process include the following:

- Using each other's goals to jointly develop a program that helps both parties' mission and goals.
- Identifying what resources each of the partners can bring to the project.
- Clearly identifying who is responsible for what.
- Setting a reasonable timeline.
- Checking in often to ensure forward progress.
- Creating a marketing/communications plan to get the word out about the project.
- Making adjustments as needed throughout the process.
- Collecting and sharing successes.
- Designing and implementing an evaluation component.

Evaluation

The evaluation portion of the project not only measures to what degree the project met its stated goals, but considers the degree to which the partnership itself was successful and worthwhile. Once the project is over, consider issues such as these:

- How did the project impact your community's teens? What is better for them now?
- Measure the success of your joint effort and to what degree it met the needs/goals you originally developed.
- Is there any potential to grow or expand the partnership?
- Take into consideration practical things, like whether or not the partner's staff are easy to work with.

OUTCOMES-BASED EVALUATION

Many partnerships and programs implemented in part through a library can benefit from an Outcomes-Based Evaluation (OBE) at the end of the program. As defined by the Institute for Museum and Library Services (IMLS), the OBE method can help libraries measure "changes in skill, knowledge, attitude, behavior, condition, or life status for program participants. . . . OBE measures the benefits to people of their library programs," and therefore the grants that the IMLS provides to the libraries.

EXAMPLE PROGRAM FROM THE IMLS WEBSITE

The following projects' goals include changing behavior and skills through project activities.

Program: Columbia County Read Together Program

Program Purpose: The Columbia County Public Library, Columbia Regional High School, Columbia County Head Start, and Columbia County Literacy Volunteers cooperate to provide story hours, literacy information, materials, and other resources to increase the time parents and other caretakers spend reading to children.

Program Services

1. Make information visits to neighborhood community centers, County Head Start programs, and Columbia High School parenting classes.
2. Provide daily story hours for parents and other caretakers and children at library and other sites.
3. Provide library cards.
4. Provide literacy counseling.
5. Connect learners with literacy tutors.
6. Provide children's and basic reader materials to meet individual needs.
7. Provide a participant readers' support network.
   o *Intended Outcomes:* Adults will read to children more often.

o *Indicators:* Number and percent of parents or other caretakers who read to children 5 times/week or more.
o *Data Source(s):* Participant interviews.
  o *Target for Change:* At the end of year one, 75% of participating parents and other caretakers will read to children in their care 5 times per week or more.

In the program above, the ultimate goal is to improve literacy in the county, but the project has chosen to measure a more immediate and related goal that provides a short-term indication of progress. That goal is frequent reading to children. Information will be collected through a survey of participants.[5]

Follow-Up

Once the project is over, it is easy to lose touch with your project partners in the rush to get to other tasks. Follow-up is a very important part of any project, however, and will help you learn from the experience and plan for the future. Here are some suggestions for a follow-up session:

- Have some kind of final meeting where feedback can be shared and future directions of the project explored. Make sure to address areas where growth is needed as well as areas of strength.
- Celebrate all that you did together. You deserve it! And celebration is very important to group morale.
- Thank your partners. A card or note thanking your partners for their contribution may sound like a small contribution, but it can make your work relationship a bit more personal, and let your partners know their work was appreciated.

---

5. Institute for Museum and Library Services, "Grant Applications—Outcomes Based Evaluations," July 29, 2014, http://www.imls.gov/applicants/basics.aspx.

EXAMPLE PARTNERSHIPS

"I have had a wonderful relationship with ShurTech Brands (owners of Duck Brand Tape). Each year they have generously provided my teens with 12 rolls to use in many of my programs! We all know how expensive duct tape is. The teens love it, too."
—Aimee Leavitt
Young Adult Coordinator
Locust Grove, Georgia

"We have a community partnership with the school district and local university. The school district now provides bus service after school to the library daily for kids to use library services. Weekly, the college provides education majors to serve as homework helpers. The project was slated for junior high students to start, but due to community input we opened it from 5th to 8th grade. It was great. We are very small but usually had between three and sometimes up to nine students getting homework help here at the library for free after school on Wednesdays."
—Julie Elmore
Library Director
Oakland City, Indiana

"We have a partnership with one local middle school in which we have a staff member who spends one day a week in their library helping the library aide and working with students to find books. We also have a

floating collection in the library. These books belong to us but are housed in the local school for students to use. We do the same thing at a local elementary school but are there four days a week. . . .

We initiated the conversation because the schools were constructing new buildings that were not within walking distance of our facility. Students from the local middle school and one local elementary school used to walk to the library once or twice a month and check out items from the library (up to 45 classes each month). Once we realized these new buildings were being built and students would no longer be walking to our facility, we worked on possible ways we could still serve the schools.

There were several meetings (I was not a part of all of them) between our director and library board and the superintendent of schools. I would say the planning took about six months before we agreed on a contract."

—Jennifer Buch
Youth Services Librarian
Port Clinton, Ohio

"The main goal of the [after-school program Project Next Generation, a partnership with local schools] is to teach teens technology. We explore different aspects, such as digital photography, stop-motion animation, green screens, movies, and digital art. The partnership is a way to get kids who don't normally have transportation to come to the library to get involved with things we're doing.

I was able to find the e-mail for the school librarian and made the initial connection that way, although we've been working together longer than this particular project. I do a lot of school visits/book talks for them as well. For this project, we communicate mainly by e-mail, but we do meet face-to-face throughout the year. Transportation has been the biggest challenge. Thankfully, the grant has enough to cover busing to and from the school. The grant renews each year, so we will continue it as long as the grant money is still there. Even when it runs out, I will try to find ways to bring similar projects to the school itself."

—Andrea Sowers
Young Adult Librarian
Joliet, Illinois

ADDITIONAL RESOURCES TO EXPLORE

- "Building Strong Partnerships with Businesses" (http://ow.ly/pNMU0)
- "Corporate Partnerships for Non-Profits: A Match Made in Heaven?" (http://www.appl.org/files/Corporate_Partnership_article-F_Thompson.pdf)
- "It Takes a Neighborhood: Purpose Built Communities and Neighborhood Transformation" (http://ow.ly/pHAtY)
- "Public Library Partnerships Which Add Value to the Community: The Hamilton Public Library Experience" (http://ow.ly/pHzRJ)

WORKS CITED

Braun, Linda W. Maureen L. Hartman, Sandra Hughes-Hassell, and Kafi Kumasi, with contributions from Beth Yoke. *The Future of Library Services for and with Teens: A Call to Action.* January 8, 2014. http://www.ala.org/yaforum/sites/ala.org.yaforum/files/content/YALSA_nationalforum_final.pdf.

Institute for Museum and Library Services. "Grant Applications—Outcomes Based Evaluations." July 29, 2014. http://www.imls.gov/applicants/basics.aspx.

Kania, John, and Mark Kramer. "Collective Impact." *Stanford Social Innovation Review* 9, no. 1 (Winter 2011). http://www.ssireview.org/articles/entry/collective_impact.

Shermer, Michael. "As Luck Would Have It." *Scientific American.* March 26, 2006. http://www.scientificamerican.com/article.cfm?id=as-luck-would-have-it.

Appendix A

YALSA's Competencies for Librarians Serving Youth: Young Adults Deserve the Best

THE COMPETENCIES

Updated January 2010

The Young Adult Library Services Association (YALSA), a division of the American Library Association (ALA) that supports library services to teens, developed these competencies for librarians who serve young adults. Individuals who demonstrate the knowledge and skills laid out in this document will be able to provide quality library service for and with teenagers. Institutions seeking to improve their overall service capacity and increase public value to their community are encouraged to adopt these competencies.

YALSA first developed these competencies in 1981, which were revised in 1998, 2003, and 2010. The competencies can be used as a tool to evaluate and improve service, a foundation for library school curriculum, a framework for staff training and a set of guiding principles for use when speaking out for the importance of services to teens in libraries. Audiences for the competencies include:

- Library educators
- School and library administrators
- Graduate students
- Young adult specialists
- School librarians
- Library training coordinators
- Public library generalists

- Human resources directors
- Non-library youth advocates and service providers

AREA I. LEADERSHIP AND PROFESSIONALISM

The librarian will be able to:

1. Develop and demonstrate leadership skills in identifying the unique needs of young adults and advocating for service excellence, including equitable funding and staffing levels relative to those provided for adults and children.
2. Develop and demonstrate a commitment to professionalism and ethical behavior.
3. Plan for personal and professional growth and career development.
4. Encourage young adults to become lifelong library users by helping them to discover what libraries offer, how to use library resources, and how libraries can assist them in actualizing their overall growth and development.
5. Develop and supervise formal youth participation, such as teen advisory groups, recruitment of teen volunteers, and opportunities for employment.
6. Model commitment to building assets in youth in order to develop healthy, successful young adults.
7. Implement mentoring methods to attract, develop, and train staff working with young adults.

AREA II. KNOWLEDGE OF CLIENT GROUP

The librarian will be able to:

1. Become familiar with the developmental needs of young adults in order to provide the most appropriate resources and services.
2. Keep up-to-date with popular culture and technological advances that interest young adults.
3. Demonstrate an understanding of, and a respect for, diverse cultural, religious, and ethnic values.
4. Identify and meet the needs of patrons with special needs.

AREA III. COMMUNICATION, MARKETING & OUTREACH

The librarian will be able to:

1. Form appropriate professional relationships with young adults, providing them with the assets, inputs and resiliency factors that they need to develop into caring, competent adults.

2. Develop relationships and partnerships with young adults, administrators and other youth-serving professionals in the community by establishing regular communication and by taking advantage of opportunities to meet in person.

3. Be an advocate for young adults and effectively promote the role of the library in serving young adults, demonstrating that the provision of services to this group can help young adults build assets, achieve success, and in turn, create a stronger community.

4. Design, implement, and evaluate a strategic marketing plan for promoting young adult services in the library, schools, youth-serving agencies and the community at large.

5. Demonstrate the capacity to articulate relationships between young adult services and the parent institution's core goals and mission.

6. Establish an environment in the library wherein all staff serve young adults with courtesy and respect, and all staff are encouraged to promote programs and services for young adults.

7. Identify young adult interests and groups underserved or not yet served by the library, including at-risk teens, those with disabilities, non-English speakers, etc., as well as those with special or niche interests.

8. Promote young adult library services directly to young adults through school visits, library tours, etc., and through engaging their parents, educators and other youth-serving community partners.

AREA IV. ADMINISTRATION

The librarian will be able to:
1. Develop a strategic plan for library service with young adults based on their unique needs.
2. Design and conduct a community analysis and needs assessment.
3. Apply research findings towards the development and improvement of young adult library services.
4. Design activities to involve young adults in planning and decision-making.
5. Develop, justify, administer, and evaluate a budget for young adult services.
6. Develop physical facilities dedicated to the achievement of young adult service goals.
7. Develop written policies that mandate the rights of young adults to equitable library service.
8. Design, implement, and evaluate an ongoing program of professional development for all staff, to encourage and inspire continual excellence in service to young adults.
9. Identify and defend resources (staff, materials, facilities, funding) that will improve library service to young adults.
10. Document young adult programs and activities so as to contribute to institutional and professional memory.
11. Develop and manage services that utilize the skills, talents, and resources of young adults in the school or community.

AREA V: KNOWLEDGE OF MATERIALS

The librarian will be able to:
1. Meet the informational and recreational needs of young adults through the development of an appropriate collection for all types of readers and non-readers.
2. Develop a collection development policy that supports and reflect the needs and interests of young adults and is consistent with the parent institution's mission and policies.

3. Demonstrate a knowledge and appreciation of literature for and by young adults in traditional and emerging formats.

4. Develop a collection of materials from a broad range of selection sources, and for a variety of reading skill levels that encompasses all appropriate formats, including, but not limited to, media that reflect varied and emerging technologies, and materials in languages other than English.

5. Serve as a knowledgeable resource to schools in the community as well as parents and caregivers on materials for young adults.

AREA VI - ACCESS TO INFORMATION

The librarian will be able to:

1. Organize physical and virtual collections to maximize easy, equitable, and independent access to information by young adults.

2. Utilize current merchandising and promotional techniques to attract and invite young adults to use the collection.

3. Provide access to specialized information (i.e., community resources, work by local youth, etc.).

4. Formally and informally instruct young adults in basic research skills, including how to find, evaluate, and use information effectively.

5. Be an active partner in the development and implementation of technology and electronic resources to ensure young adults' access to knowledge and information.

6. Maintain awareness of ongoing technological advances and how they can improve access to information for young adults.

AREA VII. SERVICES

The librarian will be able to:

1. Design, implement and evaluate programs and services within the framework of the library's strategic plan and based on the developmental needs of young adults and the public assets libraries represent, with young adult involvement whenever possible.

2. Identify and plan services with young adults in non-traditional settings, such as hospitals, home-school settings, alternative education, foster care programs, and detention facilities.
3. Provide a variety of informational and recreational services to meet the diverse needs and interests of young adults and to direct their own personal growth and development.
4. Continually identify trends and pop-culture interests of young people to inform, and direct their recreational collection and programming needs.
5. Instruct young adults in basic information gathering, research skills and information literacy skills - including those necessary to evaluate and use electronic information sources - to develop life-long learning habits.
6. Actively involve young adults in planning and implementing services and programs for their age group through advisory boards, task forces, and by less formal means (i.e., surveys, one-on-one discussion, focus groups, etc.)
7. Create an environment that embraces the flexible and changing nature of young adults' entertainment, technological and informational needs.

Teen Space Guidelines

FOREWORD

These guidelines were created in 2011 -2012 by a task force of the Young Adult Library Services Association (YALSA) with feedback from the library community achieved through a public comment period in the fall of 2011. Members of the task force were Katherine Trouern-Trend (chair), Audrey Sumser, Kathy Mahoney, Caroline Aversano, Samantha Marker, and Kimberly Bolan Cullin. YALSA's Board of Directors adopted the guidelines on May 24, 2012.

INTRODUCTION

This is a tool for evaluating a public library's overall level of success in providing physical and virtual space dedicated to teens, aged 12-18. Potential users of these national guidelines include library administrators, library trustees, teen services librarians, community members and job-seekers hoping to assess a library's commitment to teen services. Not every element of the guidelines may apply to every public library situation, but the guidelines can serve as a place to begin the conversation about what constitutes excellent public library space for teens.

Teens experience rapid physical, emotional and social changes while developing their intellectual capabilities and personal values, understanding and accepting their sexuality, and identifying their educational and occupational options. Libraries are vital to today's teens in order for them to achieve a successful transition from childhood to adulthood. They offer the resources and the environment that foster positive intellectual, emotional and social development of tomorrow's adults. All of these factors contribute to the need for distinct teen spaces, both in-library and virtually. The national guidelines that follow are intended for all library personnel working with and for teens, so they can fully understand the mission of library service to this frequently underserved age group and the importance of dedicated physical and virtual teen spaces for their continued engagement, growth and achievement.

The mission of the Young Adult Library Services Association (YALSA) is to expand and strengthen library services for teens. Through its member-driven advocacy, research, and professional development initiatives, YALSA builds the capacity of libraries and librarians to engage, serve, and empower teens and young adults. YALSA is a subspecialty of the American Library Association, the world's largest and oldest library organization, and a financially stable 501(c)3 not-for-profit.

To learn more about YALSA or to access other national guidelines relating to library services to teens, go to www.ala.org/yalsa.

GUIDELINES FOR PHYSICAL SPACE

1.0 Solicit teen feedback and input in the design and creation of the teen space.

A cornerstone of teen library services is the principle that teens must be actively involved in decisions regarding collections, services, and programs intended for them. Their active participation ensures that the evolving needs and interests of teens are being addressed, and they play a key role in attracting peers to the library. Teens become lifelong library users and supporters when they are enthusiastically engaged in planning and decision-making, and their sense of ownership will enhance the quality of their library experience.

1.1 Create a space that meets the needs of teens in the community by asking teens to play a role in the planning process.

1.2 Solicit teen feedback in the design of the space and regarding its use to allow teens to develop a sense of ownership.

1.3 Solicit teen feedback in the development of policies to ensure the space is representative of teen needs.

2.0 Provide a library environment that encourages emotional, social and intellectual development of teens.

Twenty-first century teens have an unprecedented power and enthusiasm in shaping their social and learning environments through the growth of digital communication. These tools have created new social norms and expectations for teens from diverse backgrounds. Public libraries must strive to recreate this online experience by hosting an inviting, high interest, multipurpose physical space for teens. In doing so, the library nurtures teens' values, identity, and the new skills necessary to grow and thrive. The environment should:

2.1 Convey that it is teen-owned and maintained.

2.2 Be comfortable, inviting, open and have a vibrant and teen-friendly look and feel.

2.3 Accommodate individual as well as group use for socializing and learning.

2.4 Include colorful and fun accessories selected by teens. Include up-to-date and teen friendly décor.

2.5 Allow for ample display of teen print, artistic and digital creations.

2.6 Allow food and drink in the space.

2.7 Contribute to a sense of teen belonging, community involvement, and library appreciation.

2.8 Be appealing to both users and non-users and provide resources for customers from diverse social groups, backgrounds and interests.

2.9 Be easy to navigate with clear signage and distinct areas for socializing, entertainment, teen print/digital collections and study and quiet areas.

2.10 Be easily navigable for teens with wheelchairs, walkers and other assistive devices

3.0. Provide a library space for teens that reflects the community in which they live.

Twenty-first century teens have the ability to select and engage in communities of their choice based on interest and identification with cultural, social and knowledge groups. A public library must provide a space for teens that builds upon the culture and size of the teen community and facilitates user-friendly engagement in the space. The space should:

3.1 Reflect the communities the library serves.

3.2 Be proportionate in size to the percentage of a community's teen population.

3.3 Incorporate creative design and signage to make it evident that the area is for teens.

3.4 Be designed and located to accommodate noise and activity away from quiet areas of the library and the children's area.

3.5 Provide easy access to research materials and staff assistance.

3.6 Provide separate rooms for programming and quiet study spaces.

3.7 Encourage visibility for unobtrusive staff supervision.

3.8 Accommodate a variety of uses including leisure reading, socializing, and individual and group activity.

3.9 Provide workspace for the teen librarian.

3.10 Have adequate and appropriate shelving for a diverse collection, displays and exhibit space.

3.11 Designed to be handicapped accessible and in compliance with the Americans with Disabilities Act (ADA).

4.0 Provide and promote materials that support the educational and leisure needs of teens.

According to Lee Rainie, director of the Pew Internet and American Life Project, the mobile revolution has changed people's sense of time, place and presence and has lead to a new media ecology . This sets a new standard for the expected immediacy and availability of desired information in all formats. Libraries have an important role in providing appropriate materials to help teens navigate, consume and create information for entertainment and lifelong skill development.

4.1 Ensure a teen collection development policy is in place that is aligned with the mission and goals of the library and the library's overall collection development policy.

4.2 House materials within the space that address the unique emotional, intellectual, and social maturity of middle and high-school age adolescents.

4.3 Maintain a teen collection that supports and addresses the interests and needs of teens in the community.

4.4 Maintain materials that are evaluated and weeded on a timely basis for condition and relevance.

4.5 Maintain a teen collection that includes a wide variety of formats, including but not limited to:

4.5.a. Print fiction and non-fiction

4.5.b. Music, including but not limited to CD, MP3, and other emergent technologies.

4.5.c. Video resources, including but not limited to DVD, Blu-Ray and other emergent technologies.

4.5.d. Downloadable books.

4.5.e. Downloading stations for in-library use.

4.5.f. Circulating hardware, including but not limited to laptops, eReaders, MP3 players and other emergent technologies

4.5.g. Audiobooks and other emergent technologies.

4.5.h. Graphic novels, manga, comic books, and anime.

4.5.i. Video games and gaming systems.

4.5.j. Magazines, both recreational and educational.

4.5.k. Electronic databases and other digital research materials.

4.5.l. Print research materials.

5.0 Ensure the teen space has appropriate acceptable use and age policies to make teens feel welcome and safe.

The teen space is intended for use by customers age 12-18 years old, and its purpose is to centralize the information and recreation resources of this age group while offering teens a safe, supportive, and positive space that is uniquely their own.

5.1 Actively seek teen input in the creation of the teen space guidelines, empowering the teens to serve as valuable resources.

5.2 Clearly state and display guidelines once they have been discussed and determined.

5.3   Ensure that both staff and the public are aware of the rules and expectations for using the space.

5.3   Address common points and behaviors within the guidelines, including but not limited to:

5.3.a.   Age requirement

5.3.b.   Use of appropriate language and behavior, including no fighting, no public displays of affection, and cleaning up one's mess.

5.4   Expect teens to respect themselves and the space and convey this clearly in the guidelines.

5.5   Consider adopting a "teen-only" policy for use of the space to create a space that is uniquely their own. A teen-only space can:

5.5.a.   Indicate to teens that the library cares about their unique developmental, recreational, educational, and social needs.

5.5.b.   Enable teens to be themselves in a teen-friendly environment.

5.5.c.   Help teens feel more at ease in the library.

5.5.d.   Help contain noise levels that may be distracting to other patrons.

5.5.e.   Contribute to the safety and well-being of teens while in the library.

5.6   Limit adult use of the teen-only space to browsing materials for a period of time not to exceed 15 minutes, adult tutors who are currently working with teen students, adults accompanied by a teen, and library staff. This space can:

5.6.a.   Allow teens to feel comfortable in an area where other teens are the primary occupants.

5.6.b.   Enable teens to feel safe from risky, adult-initiated interactions.

6.0 Provide furniture and technology that is practical yet adaptive.

The space is designed to accommodate a variety of activities and is flexibly arranged so these activities can take place easily. Furniture, fixtures and technology should be multifunctional and flexible so that as needs and activities change the area can be adapted accordingly. The selected furniture and fixtures should be conducive to marketing library material through displays and arrangements that stimulate discovery and use. Browsing areas for materials should encourage teens to engage in the library at their own pace and comfort level.

6.1   Have shelving for materials in various formats.

6.2   Provide comfortable and durable seating and tables for teens of all sizes and abilities. Include furniture that is wheelchair accessible.

6.3   Include furniture that is easy to move around the space in order to allow for a multitude of group, individual, and programmatic activities.

6.4   Include display equipment such as bulletin boards and display cases.

6.5   Ensure ample trash receptacles are available.

6.6   Provide a reference or information services desk or kiosk, clock, and telephone as well as ample storage for teen librarian's supplies.

6.7   Offer listening, viewing, and downloading equipment for a full range of user abilities/needs. Ensure assistive hardware and software technology is available for vision and hearing disabled teens.

6.8   Be technology rich and include both stationary and portable technology that is easily accessible and exposes teens to a diversity of hardware and software for both entertainment and learning.

6.9   Offer access to current and emerging platforms and tools, including but not limited to social networking and photo-sharing sites, user-driven communication tools for tagging and review sharing, audio and visual production technologies, and interactive Web services.

6.10 Provide adequate lighting, ventilation, temperature controls, and acoustics.

6.11 Include ample outlets to allow for technology owned by the library as well as technology owned and brought into the space by teens.

6.12 Provide adequate network infrastructure.

6.13 Ensure wireless capability.

GUIDELINES FOR VIRTUAL SPACES

7.0 Ensure content, access and use is flexible and adaptive

Online communication and engagement is central to the rhythms of teenagers' lives. Many teens have self-structured identities and social environments online and exist in a rapidly converging virtual and physical world. According to Pew researchers, three-fourths of teenagers contribute content online and are key players in the digital information revolution. Traditionally libraries have sought to push information out to library users through librarian-created content, but it is vital in today's world to recognize and adapt to the changing information needs and expectations of our teen patrons. Teens should be active participants in the creation and maintenance of the library's online presence. An attractive and functional virtual space should be designed with teen input, evaluated regularly by teens, have interactive features, and be usable on a mobile device. The virtual space should:

7.1 Support and use social media as a vital means of communication.

7.2 Allow teens to share their work, receive feedback and build community.

7.3 Model safe and appropriate use of social media tools for teens.

7.4 Support collaboration with adults and peers.

7.5 Allow administrative rights and content contribution to both library staff and teens.

7.6 Be interactive.

7.7 Support and feature mechanisms for teens to connect in real time virtually with library staff who can assist them with research needs such as chat, text message, and Skype, among others.

7.8 Support and feature mechanisms for teens to connect with one another through the library website to talk about books, homework, and research.

7.9 Support and provide capabilities for taking part in programs virtually.

7.10   Offer classes, drop-in sessions, and/or virtual instruction to educate and teach use of Web 2.0 tools and other emerging technologies.

7.11   Provide positive online interactions modeled by library staff.

7.12   Include content, photos and videos produced by teens in accordance with the library's photo release policy.

7.13   Designed to be accessible for those with visual, auditory, and motor disabilities. See The Internet and Web-based Content Accessibility Checklist (www.ala.org/ascla/asclaprotools/thinkaccessible/internetwebguidelines) provided by the Association for Specialized and Cooperative Library Agencies.

8.0 Ensure the virtual space reflects 21st century learning standards.

Through interaction and participation in digital media, teens are developing important social and technical skills helping to build a skill set necessary to learn and thrive in today's networked world. As virtual and physical worlds continue to converge, teens need tools, support and resources to harness information in a way that is meaningful to their particular needs and as participants in multiple and diverse social and learning environments.

8.1   Help teens thrive in a complex information environment.

8.2   Expose teens to diverse perspectives, gather and use information ethically and use social tools responsibly and safely.

8.3   Support the development of multiple literacies including digital, visual, textual and technological information navigation and use.

8.4   Enhance teen information literacy skills through opportunities to share and learn with others, both physically and virtually.

8.5   Teach respect for copyright and the intellectual property rights of creators and producers.

8.6   Connect understanding to the real world.

8.7   Help teens consider diverse and global perspectives.

8.8   Engage teens in social and intellectual networks of learning to gather and share information.

8.9   Use technology and other information tools to organize and display knowledge and understanding in ways that others can view, use, and assess.

8.10   Help teens connect learning to community issues.

8.11   Contribute to the exchange of ideas within and beyond the learning community.

8.12   Respect the principles of intellectual freedom.

8.13   Use creative and artistic formats to express personal learning.

9.0 Provide digital resources for teens that meet their unique and specific needs.

21st century teens interact with a range of materials in multiple formats in their school and leisure environments. According to the MacArthur Foundation, we are in the midst of a knowledge revolution that is changing how we approach learning and leisure resources for youth. Libraries need to adapt to this new paradigm and provide resources and support for teen's natural gravitation to digital media platforms.

9.1   Provide general contact information for the library and specific contact information for the teen librarian and teen content creators.

9.2   Feature information about library programs and activities for teens.

9.3   Feature a collection development policy for website content and links that includes a procedure for addressing challenges to controversial websites and a procedure for users to suggest additional electronic resources.

9.4   Feature annotated booklists and book reviews, and/or links to teen literature sites that provide reader's advisory services.

9.5   Promote teen collections and resources.

9.6   Feature informational and recreational links, including the library catalog, databases, and recreational links suggested by teens.

9.7   Feature interactive information of interest and need to teens including, but not limited to, homework help; health and sexuality; financial advice; relationship advice; time management tips; pop culture; college prep.

9.8   Provide opportunities for teens to post reviews of materials.

9.9   Provide links to the library's Teen Advisory Board blog, wiki, Twitter feed, or other means of online communication.

9.10 Feature interactive content that helps teens learn how to use library resources.

9.11 Feature content that is changed and updated frequently.

RESOURCES

While every effort has been made to ensure the accuracy of URLs in this document, please bear in mind that websites change frequently.

- American Association of School Librarians. 2007. "Standards for the 21st Century Learner." Accessed May 31, 2012. www.ala.org/aasl/sites/ala.org.aasl/files/content/guidelinesandstandards/learningstandards/AASL_LearningStandards.pdf.
- Apple in Education. "Useful to Everyone, Right from the Start." Accessed May 31, 2012. www.apple.com/education/special-education/
- Association of Specialized and Cooperative Library Agencies. 2010. "Assistive Technology: What You Need to Know." www.ala.org/ascla/sites/ala.org.ascla/files/content/asclaprotools/accessibilitytipsheets/tipsheets/11-Assistive_Technol.pdf
- Bernier, Anthony. 2010. "Spacing Out with Young Adults: Translating YA Space Concepts Back into Practice." In The Information Needs and Behaviors of Urban Teens: Research and Practice, edited by Denise E. Agosto and Sandra Hughes-Hassell, 113-126. Chicago: ALA Editions.
- Bernier, Anthony. 2010. "Ten Years of 'YA Spaces of Your Dreams': What Have We Learned?" Voice of Youth Advocates Online. Accessed May 31, 2012. www.voya.com/2010/05/13/ten-years-of-ya-spaces-of-your-dreams-what-have-we-learned.
- Bernier, Anthony. 2009. "'A Space for Myself to Go': Early Patterns in Small YA Spaces." Public Libraries 48(5): 33–47.
- Bernier, Anthony and Nicole Branch. 2009. "A TeenZone: Humming Its Own New Tune." Voice of Youth Advocates 32(3): 204–206.

- Bernier, Anthony, ed. 2012. YA Spaces of Your Dreams Collection. Bowie, Md.: VOYA Press.
- Bolan, Kimberly. 2011. "Best Practice in Teen Space Design Webinar. Accessed May 31, 2012. www.ala.org/yalsa/onlinelearning/webinars/webinarsondemand
- Bolan, Kimberly. 2008. "YALSA White Paper: The Need for Teen Spaces in Public Libraries." Accessed May 31, 2012. www.ala.org/yalsa/guidelines/whitepapers/teenspaces.
- Bolan (Taney), Kimberly. 2008. Teen Spaces: The Step-by-Step Library Makeover. Chicago: ALA Editions.
- Braun, Linda. 2010. "The Big App : New York Libraries Take Homework Help Mobile — with a Little Help from Their Friends." School Library Journal. Accessed May 31, 2012. www.schoollibraryjournal.com/slj/home/887747-312/the_big_app_new_yorks.html.csp.
- Braun, Linda. 2006. "Instant Messages." YALSABlog. Accessed May 31, 2012. http://yalsa.ala.org/blog/2006/03/12/instant-messages.
- Braun, Linda. 2010. "Whose Space Is It?" YALSABlog, Accessed May 31, 2012. http://yalsa.ala.org/blog/2010/03/05/whose-space-is-it/
- Daly, Erin. 2012. "30 Days of Innovation: Incorporate Art Into Your Teen Space." YALSABlog, Accessed May 31, 2012. http://yalsa.ala.org/blog/2012/04/11/30-days-of-innovation-11-incorporate-teen-art-into-your-space/
- Duffy, Mairead. 2012. "30 Days of Innovation #5: Changing Your Point of Reference." YALSABlog. Accessed May 31, 2012. http://yalsa.ala.org/blog/2012/04/05/30-days-of-innovation-5-changing-your-point-of-reference/
- Farrelly, Michael Garrett. 2012. Make Room for Teens: A Guide to Developing Teen Spaces in Libraries. Santa Barbara, Calif.: Libraries Unlimited.
- Feinberg, Sandra and James R Keller. 2010. Designing Space for Children and Teens in Public Spaces and Libraries. Chicago: ALA Editions.
- Fialkoff, Francine. 2010. "Third Place or Thinking Space." Library Journal. Accessed on May 31, 2012. www.libraryjournal.com/article/CA6716262.html

- Flowers, Sarah. 2010. Young Adults Deserve the Best: YALSA's Competencies in Action. Chicago : ALA Editions, 2010.
- IMLS, 2014 "Learn Labs in Libraries and Museums: Transformative Spaces for Teens." Accessed December 15, 2014. http://www.imls.gov/assets/1/AssetManager/LearningLabsReport.pdf
- Ito, Mizuko, et. al. 2009. Hanging Out, Messing Around, and Geeking Out: Kids Living and Learning with New Media. Cambridge, Mass.: MIT Press, 2009.
- Ito, Mizuko, et al. 2008. "Living and Learning with New Media : Summary of Findings from the Digital Youth Project. Accessed May 31, 2012. http://digitalyouth.ischool.berkeley.edu/files/report/digitalyouth-WhitePaper.pdf.
- Jones, Patrick, Mary K. Chelton and Joel Shoemaker. 2001. Do It Right: Best Practices for Serving Teens in School and Public Libraries. New York: Neal-Schuman.
- King, David Lee. 2011. "Content Creation, Media Labs, and Hackerspaces." David Lee King Blog. Accessed May 31, 2012. www.davidleeking.com/2011/12/15/content-creation-media-labs-and-hackerspaces/#.T8IwbZlYt2k.
- "Learning Space Toolkit." 2013. A collaboration between IMLS, North Carolina State University, brightspot, and Strategy Plus at Aecom. Accessed February 20, 2013. http://www.learningspacetoolkit.org./
- Lenhart, Amanda, et al. 2011. "Teen Kindness and Cruelty on Social Network Sites." Pew Internet and American Life Project. Accessed May 31, 2012. http://pewinternet.org/Reports/2011/Teens-and-social-media.aspx.
- Library Journal and School Library Journal. The Digital Shift: Libraries and New Media. Accessed May 31, 2012. www.thedigitalshift.com.
- Library Roadshow. 2012. "Michelle Shows Us ImaginOn's Teen Space." Video. Accessed May 31, 2012. http://youtu.be/5cubsGMSlnA.
- McGrath, Renee. 2011. "Creating a Mobile Booklist 'App.'" Young Adult Library Services 10 (2): 35–37.
- McCue, T.J. 2011. "First Public Library To Create a Maker Space." Forbes. Accessed May 31, 2012. www.forbes.com/sites/tjmccue/2011/11/15/first-public-library-to-create-a-maker-space/

- Microsoft. "Microsoft Accessibility: Technology for Everyone." Accessed May 31, 2012. www.microsoft.com/enable.
- KQED. Mind/Shift: How We Will Learn. Accessed May 31, 2012. http://blogs.kqed.org/mindshift.
- Peoski, Laura. "Where Are All the Teens? Engaging and Empowering them Online." Young Adult Library Services 8(2): 26–28.
- Rainie, Lee and Susannah Fox. 2012. "Just in Time Information through Mobile Connections." Pew Internet and American Life Project. Accessed May 31, 2012. www.pewinternet.org/Reports/2012/Just-in-time.aspx.
- Rainie, Lee. 2011. "Libraries and the New Community Information Ecology." Video presentation. Accessed May 31, 2012. www.pewinternet.org/Presentations/2011/Apr/Beyond-Books.aspx.
- Reeder, Jessica. 2011. "Are Maker Spaces the Future of Libraries." Shareable: Science & Tech. Accessed May 31, 2012. www.shareable.net/blog/the-future-of-public-libraries-maker-spaces.
- Search Institute. "Developmental Assets Lists." Accessed May 31, 2012. www.search-institute.org/developmental-assets/lists.
- Toppo, Greg. 2010. "Digital LibraryAims to Expand Kids' Media Literacy." USA Today. Accessed May 31, 2012. www.usatoday.com/news/education/story/2011-10-09/chicago-teens-build-media-literacy-in-digital-library/50714312/1.
- Watters, Audrey. 2011. "Libraries and Museums Become Hands-On Learning Labs." KQED Mind/Shift. Accessed May 31, 2012. http://blogs.kqed.org/mindshift/2011/11/libraries-and-museums-set-to-become-hands-on-learning-labs.
- YOUmedia. YOUMedia Web site. Accessed May 31, 2012. www.youmedia.org.
- Ypulse. 2010. "Ypulse Interview: Kim Bolan Cullin: 'Teen Spaces.'" Accessed May 31, 2012. www.ypulse.com/post/view/ypulse-interview-kim-bolan-cullin-teen-spaces

MODEL PHYSICAL & VIRTUAL TEEN SPACES

Library: Frankfort Community Public Library
Location: Frankfort, IN
Teen Space Name: The Edge
Virtual Space: http://fcpl.accs.net/teen.htm
Contact: Tom Smith, Assistant Director and Kirsten Weaver, Teen and
Outreach Librarian

Library: Waupaca Area Public Library
Location: Waupaca, WI
Teen Space Name: Best Cellar
Virtual Space: www.waupacalibrary.org/teens
Contact: Peg Burington, Director

Library: Newark Public Library
Location: Newark, NY
Teen Space Name: The Teen Spot
Virtual Space: http://newarklibraryteenspot.blogspot.com/
Contact: Elly Dawson, Director

Library: Plymouth District Library
Location: Plymouth, MI
Teen Space Name: Teen Zone
Virtual Space: http://plymouthlibrary.org/index.php/teen
Contact: Cathy Lichtman, Teen Service Librarian

Library: Farmington Public Library
Location: Farmington, New Mexico
Teen Space Name: Teen Zone
Virtual Space: www.infoway.org/TeenZone/index.asp
Contact: Barbara Savage Huff, Youth Services Librarian

Library: Chicago Public Libary, Harold Washington Library Center
Location: Chicago, IL
Teen Space Name: YouMedia
Virtual Space: http://youmediachicago.org/2-about-us/pages/2-about-us
Contact: Mike Hawkins, YouMedia Coordinator/Lead Mentor

Library: Tacoma Public Library
Location: Tacoma, WA
Teen Space Name: Story Lab
Virtual Space: www.storylabtacoma.org/
Contact: Sara Sunshine Holloway, Librarian

Library: Queens Library
Location #1: Queens Library for Teens, Far Rockaway, NY
Virtual Space: www.facebook.com/queenslibraryforteens
Location #2: Flushing Branch, Flushing, NY
Virtual Space #2: http://queenslibrary.org/index.aspx?page_id=44&
branch_id=F
Contact: Vikki Terrile, Coordinator of Young Adult Services

Library: Detroit Public Library
Location: Detroit, MI
Teen Space Name: H.Y.P.E. (Helping Young People Excel)
Virtual Space: http://dplhype.org
Contact: Lurine Carter, Children's and Youth Services Coordinator

Library: Orange County Library System
Location: Orlando, FL
Teen Space Name: Club Central
Virtual Space: www.ocls.info/Children/Teen/doit/club_central_do_it.asp
Contact: Vera Gubnitskaia, Youth Services Manager

Library: Gail Borden Public Library District
Location: Elgin, IL
Teen Space Name: Studio 270
Virtual Space:www.gailborden.info/m/content/view/1302/905/
Contact:Billie Jo Moffett and Melissa Lane, Studio 270 Co-Managers

Teen Programming (Draft) Guidelines*

*Final version will be published in February 2015

INTRODUCTION

These guidelines are intended to guide library staff who design, host, and evaluate library programs with and for teens. They were developed in alignment with the The Future of Library Services for and with Teens: a Call to Action, with the intention of helping library staff leverage their skills and resources to provide relevant, outcomes-based programs to better the lives of all teens in their community. While not every program will meet every guideline, library staff should strive to address most of these guidelines to be better positioned to support teens in their interests, education, skills, and relationship to their community.

Traditionally, many teens have accessed the library primarily for academic support. While these connections are important, it is crucial that youth also experience informal learning in their libraries. Technology and social media are deeply embedded in the lives of today's teens. To meet their needs, libraries must provide connected learning opportunities that are driven by teen interests and incorporate thoughtful, forward-thinking use of technology while building personal, academic, or workplace skills. Programs should promote print, digital, and media literacies, as well as soft skills such as leadership, collaboration, innovation, and critical thinking.

Libraries are in a unique position to serve as hubs, connecting residents with resources that inform and expand their interests, both inside library buildings and in the community beyond. As teens undergo physical, social, and emotional developmental changes and build their identities, they require experiences that bridge different spheres of learning.

Effective teen programs foster peer-based learning and positive developmental relationships, leverage unique library resources, and enable the acquisition of twenty-first century workforce skills.

The mission of the Young Adult Library Services Association (YALSA) is to expand and strengthen library services for teens. Through its member-driven advocacy, research, and professional development initiatives, YALSA builds the capacity of libraries and librarians to engage, serve, and empower teens and young adults. YALSA is a subspecialty of the American Library Association, a 501(c)3 organization.

To learn more about YALSA or to access other national guidelines relating to library services to teens, go to www.ala.org/yalsa/guidelines.

GUIDELINES FOR TEEN PROGRAMMING

1.0 Align programs with library and community priorities.

Before defining a teen programming plan, engage with the rest of your library and community. When teen programming relates to broader library and community-defined goals, there is a likelihood of more support as well as opportunities for funding and partnerships.

1.1   Align programming with the library's priorities, mission, and strategic plan.

1.2   When planning teen programming, consider and identify the ways in which teen programming outcomes contribute to the library's overall strategic goals.

1.2   Conduct ongoing research on priorities and projects related to youth success in your city, county, state and/or region. (For example, a mayor's office or state board of education may announce goals related to improving graduation rates, increasing the percentage of youth who continue to postsecondary education, etc.).

1.3   Have teens communicate directly with library staff, Administration, Board of Trustees, Friends groups, volunteers, and other stakeholders about the goals of teen programming, its relevance to the library's larger mission, and its positive outcomes for youth.

1.4 Continually advocate across the organization for the importance and relevance of teen programs.

1.5 When developing programs, involve cross-divisional teams and key stakeholders among library staff in order to benefit from numerous perspectives and build buy-in.

2.0 Facilitate teen-led programs.

When teens take the lead on all aspects of library programming, they grow as leaders and decision-makers, becoming more proactive, confident, and independent. This in turn adds value to the overall library program, because the library can demonstrate a role in helping teens develop key soft skills needed to be successful in school and the workplace.

2.1 Engage teens via ongoing outreach to schools, community organizations, etc.

2.2 Strive for diverse program attendance by targeting underserved teens including but not limited to youth who are low income, immigrant, LGBTQ, or of varied abilities and inviting them to be active collaborators and participants.

2.3 Involve teens in every step of the program planning process, including design, marketing, hosting, and evaluation.

2.4 Use a flexible design and action research model to allow teens to modify and adapt programs to better meet their needs.

2.5 Facilitate programs, rather than act as leader and expert.

2.6 Enable teens to engage in peer-supported learning activities.

2.7 Create an environment in which teens can collaborate and network with peers outside their own cultural group.

2.8 Balance the needs and skills of all youth program participants.

3.0 Develop interest-based, developmentally appropriate programs that support connected learning.

Each teen in the community should be able to find something in the library's menu of programs that allows them to connect to their identity and interests. Programs should be driven by teens' passions and designed to help them explore and shape their identity and skill sets, both personal and professional.

3.1 Develop programs that address the unique emotional, intellectual, and social needs of teens.

3.2 Enable teens to gain workforce development skills, including creativity, innovation, communication, and collaboration.

3.3 Enable teens to explore career pathways.

3.4 Enable teens to develop learning and innovation skills, such as critical thinking and problem solving, media literacy, digital literacy, and information and communication technologies literacy.

3.5 Incorporate technology and social media intelligently and organically.

3.6 Connect youth with mentors, guides, and other adult role models and educators.

3.7 Connect youth with opportunities to become civically engaged.

3.8 Incorporate a variety of types of interaction, such as one-on-one engagement, small group discussion or activities, and large events.

3.9 Enable teens to demonstrate proficiency in non-traditional media and platforms.

3.10 Enable teens to engage in self-expression and meaningful content creation.

4.0. Create programming that reflects the needs and identities of all teens in the community.

In order to ensure that library programming meets the needs of all members of the community and does not duplicate services provided elsewhere, library staff should have a thorough understanding of the communities they serve. Library staff must continually analyze their communities so that they have current knowledge about demographics and trends. They must also develop relationships with community organizations already working with youth. Library staff play a crucial role in connecting teens to the community agencies and individuals that can best meet their needs.

4.1 Identify any demographic information that has already been gathered by library staff.

4.2   Regularly collect available demographic information from the census, public schools data, local government agencies, etc.

4.3   Continually identify segments of the community that are underserved by library programming.

4.4   Continually identify other agencies and organizations that are already serving teens and families.

4.5   Determine which teen needs are being met by programming and services at other organizations.

4.6   Build strong relationships with community leaders at these organizations and refer teens as appropriate.

4.7   Direct the library's limited resources appropriately to provide needed programming that is relevant to local teens, reflective of their identities and interests, and not already offered elsewhere.

5.0 Develop rich, mutually beneficial community partnerships.

Library staff must develop programming in partnership with other organizations in order to effectively serve all teens in the community. By working with partners, libraries reach new audiences, create robust and relevant programs that truly reflect the community, and leverage a host of resources to meet the needs of youth and families. A partnership can begin many ways—an email, a phone call, a visit, or an introduction by another community partner.

5.1   Regularly assess existing community contacts and library partnerships to consider how they may be maintained or expanded.

5.2   Regularly seek out new community partners (government agencies, community organizations, vocational programs, etc.) who target a teen audience the library would like to reach (e.g., homeless or low income youth) and/or have skills or access to resources that would benefit teens.

5.3   At initial meetings, listen carefully to the community group's goals, objectives, and areas of need.

5.5   Establish a mutually beneficial relationship in which the library and the community organization participate as equals.

5.6   Create a written agreement or memorandum of understanding that explicitly states what each partner is contributing, how each will benefit from the relationship, and how success will be measured.

5.7 Develop programming that best utilizes partner and library resources to meet the needs of teens and achieve shared goals.

5.8 Establish an ongoing dialog between partners, budgeting time to debrief, celebrate success, learn from failure, and otherwise maintain the overall health of the partnership.

5.9 As appropriate, host programs in partner locations (e.g., youth homeless shelters, community centers, classrooms, etc.) in order to serve teens where they are and increase the visibility of the library.

5.10 Work collaboratively with community partners to develop and administer an outcomes-based evaluation.

5.11 Continue to refine jointly offered programs based on evaluations and feedback.

6.0 Staff programs sufficiently and appropriately.

Programs should be adequately staffed to ensure the safety and enjoyment of participants. Consideration should be given to the size of the space, expected attendance, and the complexity of the program.

6.1 Ensure that staffing levels are adequate to creating a secure and welcoming environment.

6.2 Ensure that staff/patron ratios are adequate to allow for successful programs.

6.3 Consider which tasks are best suited to librarians and which are more suited to paraprofessional staff, community partners, mentors, teen volunteers, participants, etc.

6.4. Consider the needs of teen participants (language, culture, ability, etc.) and staff programs accordingly.

6.5. When hosting programs led by outside facilitators/presenters, consider ways to ensure that teens also develop positive relationships with library staff.

7.0 Provide targeted and ongoing training to staff who host teen programs.

Library staff who plan and host programming for and with teens should adopt YALSA's Competencies for Librarians Serving Youth, particularly those related to Client Knowledge and Services. Areas of focus are outlined below. Staff training should be regular and ongoing.

7.1   Train library staff in facilitation and power sharing, including working with teens to set and manage behavior expectations.

7.2   Train staff in cross-cultural functioning and communication to effectively serve teens of all backgrounds, abilities, orientations, and identities.

7.3   Train staff in public speaking, collaboration, partnership-building, supervision, outcome measurement, advocacy, and project management.

7.4   Train staff to use technology effectively.

7.5   Train staff on key documents such as the 40 Developmental Assets for Adolescents, and to consider which Assets each program will advance.

7.6   Continuously share training and professional development resources among all library staff to ensure positive and meaningful interactions with teens, both during and after programs.

8.0 Host programs in spaces that support the engagement, growth, and achievement of teens.

Teen programs should be held in spaces that are comfortable, inviting, and meet the purposes of each program.

8.1   When hosting programs inside the library building and/or as part of the library's online presence, consult YALSA's Teen Space Guidelines.

8.2   Alert colleagues who are not directly involved with programming when programs are scheduled and what they will involve (equipment, noise levels, food/drink, etc.).

8.3   When programs are hosted outside the library in a community partner's space, have conversations in advance to create shared expectations and goals (see section 4.0 for more on partnerships).

8.4   For programs hosted in a partner's space, take steps to highlight the collaboration and the library's role in the program. These steps might include but are not limited to:

8.4 a.   Having the community partner and library staff member jointly announce that the program is a collaboration, with each partner highlighting the other's contribution.

8.4.b.   Posting co-branded signage.

8.4.c.   Checking out materials or showcasing library resources onsite.

8.4.d.   Creating new library accounts onsite.

8.4.e.   Documenting the program via photos, audio and/or video for the online and social media presence of the library and partner.

9.0 Develop appropriate and welcoming policies.

Library staff must ensure that teens of all abilities, income levels, sexual orientations, gender identities, ethnic and religious groups, and other underrepresented groups feel safe and welcome at library programs.

9.1   Facilitate a conversation with teens to allow them to create behavior expectations that foster a safe environment for discussing personal or controversial topics, as appropriate.

9.2   Clearly state the intended audience for programs, and ensure that discussions and activities are age-appropriate.

9.3   Advocate for, establish, and adhere to general library policies that support developmentally appropriate teen behavior at programs and in the library.

10.0 Engage in evidence-based practice and outcome measurement.

Attendance must not be the only measure of a program's success. Instead, evaluations must measure positive outcomes for participants. Programming should be fluid and flexible, undertaken with the expectation that there will be some failure, adjustments will be made, and evaluation will be ongoing.

10.1   Provide tools for teen participants to measure the effectiveness of the program, both in the moment and in the longer term.

10.2   Create evaluations that predict and measure an improvement or expansion of knowledge, skills, confidence, attitude, or behavior.

10.3   Create evaluations that predict and measure impact on the community.

10.4   Conduct evaluations often, and recalibrate programming as needed.

10.5   Continually assess the evaluation tools themselves to make sure they are adequately measuring desired outcomes. Redesign tools as needed.

10.5   Use evaluation findings to guide future planning and budget-making.

10.6.   Use evaluation findings to communicate success to key stakeholders in the library and in the community. Advocate for the ongoing need for high quality teen programming within the library and to policy makers.

RESOURCES

1.0 Situate teen programs within the broader goals of the library and the community.

- Braun, Linda, et al. 2014. "The Future of Library Services for and with Teens: A Call to Action." Accessed September 20, 2014. http://www.ala.org/yaforum/future-library-services-and-teens-project-report.
- Comito, Lauren and Franklin Escobedo. 2011. "Teens As Advocates." Young Adult Library Services. 10(1) 16-17.
- Hartman, Maureen. 2012. "Good Teen Librarians Make Great Library Advocates." Young Adult Library Services. 11(1): 10-12.
- King, Krista. 2012. "Advocacy, Teens, and Strategic Planning." Young Adult Library Services. 11(1) 24-26.
- Kordeliski, Amanda. "A Call to Action: Creating Conversations in Your State Using the YALSA Futures Report." Young Adult Library Services. 13(1): 7-10.

2.0 Facilitate teen-led programs.

- Adlawan, Lana. 2013. "Sacramento Teens Shape Their Future, One Photo and Post at a Time." Young Adult Library Services 11(2) 28-30.
- Birch, Jennifer. 2014. "Five Ideas for Using Instagram In the Library." Voice of Youth Advocates. 37(3): 32.
- England, Megan. 2014. "Creating teen leadership opportunities: a blueprint for boosting your Teen Advisory Group." Young Adult Library Services 12(3): 8-11.
- Lewis, Courtney. "Seek the Unknown for Teen Read Week 2013: Using Action Research to Determine Recreational Reading Habits of High School Students." 2013. Accessed October 7, 2014. http://www.yalsa.ala.org/yals/wp-content/uploads/2013/10/11n4_summer2013.pdf.
- Matthias, Cynthia, and Christy Mulligan. 2010. "Hennepin County Library's Teen Tech Squad." Young Adult Library Services. 8(2):13-6.
- Tuccillo, Diane P. 2009. *Teen-Centered Library Service: Putting Youth Participation into Practice.* Santa Barbara, Ca.: Libraries Unlimited.

3.0 Develop interest-based, developmentally appropriate programs that support connected learning.

- Alessio, Amy J. and Kimberly A. Patton. 2011. *A Year of Programs For Teens 2.* Chicago: ALA.
- Alexander, Linda B. and Kwon, Nahyun, 2010. *Multicultural Programs for Tweens and Teens.* Chicago: ALA Editions.
- Arnold, Mandy. 2014. "Connecting Teens To Community Service Opportunities." Voice of Youth Advocates. 37(3): 30-31.
- Balducci, Tiffany and Brianne Wilkins-Bester. 2014. *The Tween Scene: The ABCs of Library Programming for Ages 10-14.* VOYA Press.
- Bannon, Brian. 2012. "YOUmedia Chicago: connecting youth through public libraries." National Civic Review 101(4):33.
- Barak, Lauren. 2013. "Using Social Media to Engage Teens in the Library." School Library Journal Blog: The Digital Shift. Accessed October 11, 2014. http://www.thedigitalshift.com/2013/06/k-12/talking-teen-engagement-a-unique-forum-brings-together-diverse-ideas-on-using-social-media-to-reach-teens/

- Behen, Linda D. 2013. *Recharge Your Library Programs With Pop Culture And Technology: Connect With Today's Teen*. Santa Barbara, Ca.: Libraries Unlimited.
- Blakemore, Sarah-Jayne. (2012, September 17). *The mysterious workings of the adolescent brain*. Accessed September 20, 2014. https://www.youtube.com/watch?v=6zVS8HIPUng.
- Connected Learning Alliance. "Why Connected Learning?" Accessed October 12, 2014. http://clalliance.org/why-connected-learning/
- Digital Literacy Portal. Accessed October 13, 2014. http://www.ictliteracy.info/
- Dillon, Stacey and Amy Laughlin. "Starting From Scratch." School Library Journal 60(8).
- Fink, Megan, 2011. *Teen Read Week and Teen Tech Week: Tips and Resources for YALSA's Initiatives*. Chicago: YALSA.
- Ito, Mizuko and Crystle Martin. 2013. "Connected Learning and the Future of Libraries." Young Adult Library Services 12(1): 29-32.
- Ito, Mizuko, et. al. 2013. "Connected Learning: An Agenda for Research and Design." Accessed September 20, 2014. http://dmlhub.net/publications/connected-learning-agenda-research-and-design.
- Ito, Mizuko, et. al. 2009. *Hanging Out, Messing Around, and Geeking Out: Kids Living and Learning with New Media*. Cambridge, Mass.: MIT Press, 2009.
- Ito, Mizuko, et al. 2008. "Living and Learning with New Media: Summary of Findings from the Digital Youth Project. Accessed May 31, 2012.
- http://digitalyouth.ischool.berkeley.edu/files/report/digitalyouth-WhitePaper.pdf.
- Mack, Candice. 2014. "How to Host a Teen Soldering Program Without Getting Burned." Young Adult Library Services. 12(4): 16-18.
- Martin, Crystle. 2014. "Connecting Youth Interests Via Libraries." Connected Learning Research Network Blog. Accessed October 12, 2014. http://clrn.dmlhub.net/content/connecting-youth-interests-via-libraries

- McDonald, Nicola. 2014. "Mentoring Teens in Libraries." Voice of Youth Advocates. 37(2):30.
- Mulder, Natalie. 2011. "Encouraging Community Service in the Public Library." *Young Adult Library Services* 10(1): 25-7.
- Ludwig, Sarah. 2011. *Starting from Scratch: Building a Teen Library Program*. Santa Barbara, Ca.: Libraries Unlimited.
- Paul, Annie Murphy. 2014. "How Computer Coding Can Increase Engagement, Provide A Purpose For Learning." The Hechinger Report. Accessed October 11, 2014. http://hechingerreport.org/content/computer-coding-can-increase-engagement-provide-pur-pose-learning_17457/
- Rassette, Eden J. 2014. "Teens Serving Libraries." Voice of Youth Advocates. 37(2): 24.
- Search Institute. "40 Developmental Assets for Adolescents." Accessed September 20, 2014.
- http://www.search-institute.org/content/40-developmental-assets-adolescents-ages-12-18.
- Search Institute. 2014. "Developmental Relationships." Accessed October 14, 2014. http://www.search-institute.org/what-we-study/developmental-relationships
- Starkey, Monique Delatte, 2013. *Practical Programming: The Best of YA-YAAC*. Chicago: YALSA.
- Watkins, S. Craig. "Rapid Tech Change Requires Rebranding to Recruit Talent." Connected Learning Research Network Blog. Accessed October 12, 2014. http://clrn.dmlhub.net/content/rapid-tech-change-requires-rebranding-to-recruit-talent
- Weinberg, Kathie. "Financial Boot Camp for Girls." Voice of Youth Advocates. 36(5): 32.
- Williams, Tiffany. 2014. "Why Should Libraries Care About Teens And Technology?" Young Adult Library Services. 12(2): 9-12.
- Wurl, Jody. "Connected Learning and the Library: An Interview With Kristy Gale." Young Adult Library Services. 12(4): 19-21.

4.0. Create programming that reflects the needs and identities of all teens in the community.

- Barnard, Madalene Rathbun. 2013. "Color outside the library lines: serving NVLD and Asperger Syndrome teens." Voice of Youth Advocates 36(5): 28.
- Fargo, Hailley. 2014. "Using Technology To Reach At-Risk Teens." YALSAblog. Accessed October 13, 2014. http://yalsa.ala.org/blog/2014/09/26/using-technology-to-help-at-risk-teens/
- Fesko, Sharon. 2012. "Teens Reach Out Through Outreach." Voice of Youth Advocates. 35(5): 444.
- Jones, Jami L. 2009. "Shelters From the Storm: Teens, Stress, and Libraries." Young Adult Library Services. 7(2): 16-20.
- Klor, Ellin and Sarah Lapin. 2011. *Serving Teen Parents: From Literacy To Life Skills*. San Francisco: Libraries Unlimited.
- Naidoo, Jami Campell and Luis Francisco Vargas. 2011. "Libraries Bridging the Borderlands: Reaching Latino Tweens and Teens with Targeted Programming and Collections." Young Adult Library Services. 9(4): 13-30.
- Vogel, Victoria. 2008. "Library Outreach to Teens with Physical Challenges." Young Adult Library Services. 7(1): 39-42.

5.0 Develop rich, mutually beneficial community partnerships.

- Craig, Angela. 2010. "High Impact Partnership: Serving Youth Offenders." Young Adult Library Services. 9(1): 20-22.
- Farmer, Lesley. 2014. "Team Up For College Readiness." School Library Journal 60(10).
- Figel, Nancy and Renee Numeier. 2013. "Collaboration of Two Libraries For One Community's Students." Voice of Youth Advocates. 36(4): 27.
- Milazzo, Molly. 2013. "Teaming up for teens, jobs, and resources: one high school, one public library, one program." Voice of Youth Advocates. 36(5): 26.
- Pandora, Cherie P. and Stacey Hayman. 2013. *Better Serving Teens Through School Library-Public Library Collaboration*. Santa Barbara, Ca.: Libraries Unlimited.

- Rovatti-Leonard, Angela. "The Mobile LAM (Library, Archive & Museum): New Space for Engagement." Young Adult Library Services 12(2): 16-18, 21.
- Rutherford, Dawn. 2010. "Building Strong Community Partnerships: Sno-Isle and the Teen Project." Young Adult Library Services. 9(1): 23-25.
- Shelton, Jama and Julie Winkelstein. 2014. "Librarians and Social Workers: Working Together for Homeless LGBTQ Youth." Young Adult Library Services. 13(1): 20-24.
- Strock, Adrienne L. 2014. "Reaching Beyond Library Walls: Strengthening Services and Opportunities through Partnerships and Collaborations." 13(1): 15-17.

6.0 Staff programs sufficiently and appropriately.

- Steele, K-Fai. 2014. "The Future of Libraries and Nontraditional Staffing Models." Young Adult Library Services. 13(1): 11-14.

7.0 Provide targeted and ongoing training to staff who host teen programs.

- Treude, Dawn. 2013. "Lean on Me? Finding Training and Support for School Library Support Staff." Young Adult Library Services. 11(4): 4-7.
- YALSA's Competencies for Librarians Serving Youth: Young Adults Deserve the Best. Accessed November 23, 2014. http://www.ala.org/yalsa/guidelines/yacompetencies2010
- YALSA. Webinars on Demand: Programming. Accessed October 11, 2014. http://www.ala.org/yalsa/onlinelearning/webinars/webinarsondemand#program

8.0 Host programs in spaces that support the engagement, growth, and achievement of teens.

- YALSA. National Teen Space Guidelines. Accessed October 7, 2014. http://www.ala.org/yalsa/guidelines/teenspaces

9.0 Develop appropriate and welcoming policies.
- Flowers, Sarah. 2011. *Young Adults Deserve The Best: YALSA's Competencies in Action.* American Library Association.
- YALSA Training Kit: Young Adults Deserve the Best: Understanding Teen Behavior. http://www.alastore.ala.org/detail. aspx?ID=3992 Accessed 12/3/14

10.0 Engage in evidence-based practice and outcome measurement.
- Braun, Linda. 2014. "Back to School: Learning How to Fail." YALSAblog. Accessed October 14, 2014. http://yalsa.ala.org/ blog/2014/08/29/back-to-school-learning-how-to-fail/
- Dubois, David, et. al. "From Soft Skills to Hard Data: Measuring Youth Program Outcomes." The Forum For Youth Investment, January 22, 2014. Accessed October 9, 2014. http://forumfyi.org/ content/soft-skills-hard-data-
- Flowers, Sarah, 2012. *Evaluating Teen Services and Programs.* Chicago: YALSA.
- Gennett, Johannah. 2014. "Measuring Outcomes for Teen Technology Programs." Young Adult Library Services. 13(1): 25-28.
- Gordon, Carol. 2006. "A Study of a Three-Dimensional Action Research Training Model for School Library Programs." School Library Media Research: Research Journal of the American Association of School Librarians. Accessed October 11, 2014. http://bit.ly/1vOfW6u.
- Harris, Erin. (2011, December 12) "Afterschool Evaluation 101: How to Evaluate an Expanded Learning Program." Accessed October 9, 2014. http://www.hfrp.org/out-of-school-time/publications-resources/afterschool-evaluation-101-how-to-evaluate-an-expanded-learning-program.
- Pavis, April Layne. 2013. "Teen tXperts: An Evaluation." Young Adult Library Services. 11(2): 25-27.
- Ryan, Sara. 2013. "Getting Out From Under the Radar: Using YALSA's Teen Services Evaluation Tool." Young Adult Library Services 12(1): 13-15.
- Steele, K-F. 2013. "'What We Think Actually Matters?' Teen Participatory Design and Action Research at the Free Library of Philadelphia." Young Adult Library Services 11(4): 12-5.

The Future of Library Services for and with Teens: A Call to Action Executive Summary

D

LIBRARIES PROVIDE A lifeline for teens, their families and communities across the nation by providing a safe and supervised space for adolescents to engage in creative, educational activities with caring adults and mentors. But a variety of significant developments point to a need for libraries to change in order to successfully meet the needs of today's teens.

The Future of Library Services for and with Teens: a Call to Action is the result of a yearlong national forum conducted by the Young Adult Library Services Association (YALSA) in 2013, with funding provided by the Institute of Museum and Library services. The *Call to Action* lays out a new path for serving 21st century teens through libraries. This 2014 report shows that many libraries are continuing to grapple with diminishing resources while at the same time struggling to meet the needs of a changing teen population. Additionally, significant developments in technology have led to the need to rethink how services for and with teens are best created and delivered. The *Call to Action* provides recommendations on how libraries must address challenges and re-envision their teen services in order to meet the needs of their individual communities and to collectively ensure that the nation's 40+ million teens develop the skills they need to be productive citizens.

THE ISSUES

Teens Make Up a Significant Portion of Library Users
There are over 40 million adolescents, aged 12–17, living in the United States today, and they use libraries. A 2013 Pew survey found that 72% of 16- to 17-year-olds had used a public library in 2012.

Library Services and Resources for Teens Are in Jeopardy
Library closures, reduced hours, lack of staff, and insufficient resources mean that teens in many communities no longer have access to the resources, knowledge, and services they need to support their academic, emotional, and social development, to master 21st-century skills, and to ensure that they become productive citizens.

There Has Been a Significant Shift in the Demographics of Teens
According to an analysis of the 2010 census data completed by the Annie E. Casey Foundation, there are currently 74.2 million children under the age of eighteen in the United States; 46% of them are children of color. Additionally, more than one-fifth of America's children are immigrants or children of immigrants. Now is the time for the field of librarianship, the population of which is overwhelmingly Caucasian, to consider what these demographic changes mean to school and public library services and programs for and with teens.

Technology Continues to Impact Communication Methods, Teaching, and Learning
Teens' use of technology (smart phones, tablets, laptops, the Internet, etc.) is pervasive. However, ownership of technology devices continues to vary across socioeconomic and racial demographics. Now is the time for public and school libraries to systematically determine how technology will affect the future of library services for and with teens, with special attention to the access gaps that continue to exist.

Teens Are Entering the Workforce without Critical Skills
In the last three decades, the skills required for young adults to succeed in the workforce have changed drastically, but the skills emphasized in

schools have not kept up with these changes. Libraries need to create the kind of spaces, services, and opportunities that today's teens need in order to succeed in school and in life.

THE PARADIGM SHIFT AND LIBRARIES

Several important factors have come together in such a way that libraries are experiencing a seismic shift. Ever since computers entered library spaces, public and school libraries have been on a precipice of change. The library can no longer be viewed as a quiet place to connect to physical content. Instead it needs to evolve into a place, physical and virtual, where individuals can learn how to connect and use all types of resources, from physical books to apps to experts in a local, regional, or national community. Libraries must leverage new technologies and become kitchens for "mixing resources" in order to empower teens to build skills, develop understanding, create and share, and overcome adversity. In addition to the impact of new technologies, the definition of literacy has expanded beyond the cognitive ability to read and write, to a recognition that literacy is a social act that involves basic modes of participating in the world. New research also points to a concept of connected learning, in which studies show that young people learn best when that learning is connected to their passions, desires, and interests.

WHAT TEENS NEED FROM LIBRARIES

Bridge the growing digital and knowledge divide

School and public libraries must ensure that in addition to providing access to digital tools, that they also provide formal and informal opportunities for teens to learn to use them in meaningful and authentic ways.

Leverage Teens' Motivation to Learn

Too often teens' desire to learn is thwarted by an educational system too focused on testing, unwilling to adopt culturally relevant pedagogy, or so strapped for funding that only basic resources are available. Libraries live outside of a school's formal academic achievement sphere and offer a space where interest based learning can occur in a risk-free environment. Public and school libraries, therefore, need to embrace their role as both formal and informal learning spaces.

Provide Workforce Development Training

In order to address the growing need for a skilled workforce, school and public libraries have the responsibility to enable teens to learn in relevant, real world 21st century contexts.

Serve as the Connector between Teens and other Community Agencies

Libraries are only one of many organizations with a vision to build better futures for teens. Too often, however, teens are unaware of the services offered in their communities. As many of today's teens are faced with serious social and economic challenges, libraries must provide teens the assistance they need.

IMPLICATIONS FOR LIBRARIES

In order to meet the needs of today's teens and to continue to provide value to their communities, libraries need to revisit their fundamental structure, including these components:

Audience

The focus is on serving all teens in the community, not just those who are regular users of the physical library space

Collections

Are tailored to meet the unique needs of the teens in the particular community they serve, and are expanded to include digital resources as well as experts and mentors

Space
A flexible physical library space that allows for teens to work on a variety of projects with each other and adult mentors to create and share content. Virtual spaces also allow for teens to connect with each other and with experts. Libraries recognize that teens need and want to make use of the entire library space or site, not just a designated teen area.

Programming
Programs occur year-round, leverage the unique attributes of libraries, allow for teens to gain skills through exploration of their interests and measure outcomes in terms of knowledge gained or skills learned.

Staffing
Degreed library professionals focus on developing and managing teen services at the programmatic level, while face-to-face encounters are made up of a hybrid of staff and skilled volunteers who act as mentors, coaches, and connectors

Youth participation
Is integrated throughout the teen services program and enables teens to provide both on-the-fly and structured feedback for the library staff. Teen participation is not limited to formally organized groups

Outreach
Is on-going and occurs in order to identify the needs of teens in the community and then work with partners to alleviate those needs.

Policy
Focuses on serving teens no matter where they are. The policies are flexible and easy to update in order to reflect changing needs

Professional development
Takes a whole library/whole school approach to planning, delivering and evaluating teen services. Investigates attributes and resources unique to libraries and identifies means for leveraging those to achieve library goals.

Today's 40+ million adolescents face an increasing array of social issues, barriers, and challenges that many of them are unable to overcome on their own. With nearly 7,000 teens dropping out of high school per day, and approximately 40% of high school graduates not proficient in traditional literacy skills, the nation is in danger of losing an entire generation, which in turn will lead to a shortage of skilled workers and engaged citizens. Now is the time for public and school libraries to join with other key stakeholders and take action to help solve the issues and problems that negatively impact teens, and ultimately the future of the nation. These challenges are not insurmountable. It is a moral imperative for libraries to leverage their skills and resources to effect positive change and better the lives of millions of teens. In turn, libraries will be providing an invaluable service to their community and position themselves as an indispensable community resource.

More information about the initiative, as well as a digital download of the full report can be found at www.ala.org/yaforum/project-report.

E

TEEN READ WEEK™ PROGRAM PLANNING WORKSHEET

LIBRARY:
_____

PRIMARY ORGANIZER:
_____

PROGRAM TITLE:
_____

BRIEF DESCRIPTION OF PROGRAM:

PURPOSE/GOAL OF PROGRAM:

LEARNING OUTCOMES:
(what skills or knowledge will the tween/teen participants come away with?)

DATE: _____   **DAY OF WEEK:** _____

START TIME: _____   **END TIME:** _____

_____ Date checked on library calendar
_____ Date checked on school calendar
_____ Date checked on community calendar

LOCATION FOR PROGRAM:
Library meeting room   YA area   Other

TARGET AUDIENCE:
Tweens   Teens   Parents/Caregivers   All

ESTIMATED ATTENDANCE:
Tweens _____ Teens _____ Parents/Caregivers _____

PARTNERS/COSPONSORS:

YOUTH PARTICIPATION:
(what role—formal or informal--will the TAG, teen volunteers or other teens play?)

BUDGET FOR PROGRAM PROPOSAL
(estimated costs):

- Speaker's expenses (fee, travel, meals, other)
- Supplies and equipment (materials, purchases, rentals, other)
- Refreshments (incl. paper products)
- Collection development (books & other materials to support/ enhance the program)
- Staff time (organizer's hours x wage, PR staff hours x wage)
- Public relations (fliers, poster, bookmarks, press releases, mailings, postage)
- Swag (prizes, incentives, giveaways, door prizes)
- Other costs (e.g. security or police for traffic detail)

FUNDING SOURCE:

_____ Budget line- general revenue

_____ Grant funds (check www.ala.org/teenread to see if TRW grants

_____ are available)

_____ Friends of the Library

_____ Corporate sponsorship

_____ Outside donations

_____ Other

PROGRAM APPROVAL:

_____ Approved by supervisor

_____ Approved by director

_____ Off desk planning time approved, if appropriate

EQUIPMENT & SUPPLIES NEEDED:

(make arrangements to rent, if necessary)

SPEAKER CONFIRMATION:

_____ Contract sent

_____ Contract returned and executed

_____ Directions sent

_____ Follow-up call(s)

ROOM SET-UP:

(preliminary plan)

_____ Discussed with Maintenance Staff

Person(s) responsible: _____

REFRESHMENTS:

Person(s) responsible _____

PUBLICITY AND PROMOTION:

_____ Publicity materials translated into predominant language(s) of community members

_____ Teen Read Week logo downloaded and used on web site and publicity materials

_____ Requested free teen reading &/or YALSA materials via www. ala.org/yalsa/handouts

_____ Ordered Teen Read Week posters, bookmarks, etc. from www. alastore.ala.org

_____ Read through publicity ideas on www.ala.org/teenread

_____ All library staff informed and encouraged to support the effort

_____ Program information posted to library website, Facebook page, at circulation desk, etc.

_____ Fliers distributed to schools, community groups, homeschoolers, businesses and other libraries

_____ Media releases to local newspapers, school papers, radio, TV, Friends of the Library newsletter, etc.

_____ Visits to schools or community groups planned and approved

_____ Book displays set up

_____ Emails, Tweets &/or direct mailings to teens, parents, schools and community organizations

_____ Community VIPs invited (elected officials, policy makers, Foundation staff, etc.)

Person(s) responsible: _____

ACCOMPANYING RESOURCES

(choose all that apply):

_____ Exhibits

_____ Displays

_____ Handouts

_____ Bibliographies (book lists, video lists, etc.)

_____ Official TRW products from ALA Graphics

_____ Other: _____

Person(s) responsible: _____

ADVOCACY TIE-INS

_____ Invited local officials, policy makers &/or VIPs to attend

_____ Recruited a local official, policy maker &/or VIP to participate in the event (judge a contest, emcee the event, give a brief
speech, etc.)

_____ Asked the local town council &/or school board to officially
declare the week Teen Read Week in my town or school (see
resources at www.ala.org/teenread)

_____ Mailed local officials, policy makers &/or VIPs Happy Teen
Read Week cards (made by your teen patrons, perhaps)

_____ Other: _____

Person(s) responsible: _____

FINAL PROGRAM CHECKLIST:

_____ Room set-up completed

_____ Volunteers/staff helpers/TAG prepped & assigned tasks

_____ Equipment and supplies ready

_____ Refreshments procured

_____ Speaker's introduction prepared

_____ Speaker's check/stipend on hand, if appropriate

_____ Evaluation form and pencils available

_____ Fliers for next program available

_____ Parking lot details worked out

_____ Someone assigned to take photos

_____ Accommodations made for any special needs participants

_____ Link to online vote for next Teen Read Week theme posted on web site, Facebook, etc.

_____ Evaluation tools & method determined and any necessary surveys etc. are created

_____ Other: _____

FOLLOW UP CHECKLIST:

_____ Room clean up

_____ Event photos &/or summary posted online & sent to local paper

_____ Dated/time sensitive promotional posters, etc. taken down in library & removed from web site

_____ Thank you notes sent to volunteers, key staff, speaker, sponsors, etc.

_____ Evaluation forms collected and analyzed

_____ Debrief with key staff, supervisor and TAG

_____ Evaluation completed and results shared with coworkers, supervisor & stakeholders

_____ Other: _____

REFLECTION:
Was the program a success? Why or why not?

To what degree were the learning outcomes met?

What impact did this program have? (on participants, on the community, on the library)

What was the estimated attendance?

Did you encounter any unforeseen problems? How can we better prepare in the future?

What future recommendations or best practices do you want to share?

Appendix F

50+ Promotional and Public Relations Ideas to Market Programs and Services to Young Adults in Your Community

IN THE LIBRARY AND COMMUNITY

- stuff fliers into related books on a thematic display in the library
- mail or email a YA newsletter or flier to past program participants (keep your attendance logs or registration sign-up sheets)
- send fliers, handbills, or posters to other neighboring libraries
- for writing contests, keep a binder of entries and winners on display in the YA Area throughout year or post them online
- ask the local book store to distribute fliers or post information on their web site or Facebook page
- ask local places of worship to distribute fliers to their youth groups
- write an article for your library's Friends of the Library newsletter, or e-news
- hang posters at related businesses (e.g., camera shops for a photography workshop or contest)
- ask the businesses that have sponsored things like incentive prizes for the library programs or given funds to underwrite programs to put up posters or distribute fliers
- submit an article to the arts council or other community agencies' newsletters
- put a display in the glass display case in the library (e.g., sample of craft to be made at craft workshop, along with related items and books)

- promote the program on radio or television (e.g., be interviewed on public service programs, have teens make public service announcements [PSAs] to be broadcast)
- call kids directly to invite them to participate
- hang posters in schools, libraries, malls, and favorite eating places of teens
- write newspaper articles for pre- and post-publicity
- personally recruit regular library users
- get referrals from Teen Advisory Group members
- send newsletters to youth group leaders (youth directors or ministers, GS, BSA) and/or direct mailing to these adults
- send articles to locally-produced magazines for parents
- send notices for use in bulletins at places of worship (especially for family programs)
- send a direct mailing or e-blast to past summer reading/learning participants
- get into community events calendars and vacation guides
- send information to cable TV community bulletin board
- have a booth at summer information fair for recreation or summer camp opportunities
- buy an ad in recreation or other town department flier
- have mini-displays with fliers on circulation desk
- use community bulletin boards in stores and post offices
- ask to use the announcement board on fire hall's lawn
- put articles in the community newsletter via town supervisor's office
- submit an article in recreation department's newsletter
- mail a letter and fliers to community interest groups (e.g., promote a drama program to community theatre groups)
- include program information in library system's public relations calendar
- place a paid display ad in weekly "shopper" (advertising circular)
- submit an article to the library system newsletter at alert other staff to the program opportunity
- have a booth or library display at community events and fairs

- Tweet announcements out regularly and use appropriate hashtags. Ask your Teen Advisory Group members to leverage their social media accounts to spread the word.
- Post announcements on the library's Facebook page or web site
- Create a Google calendar and link to it from the library's web site, e-newsletters, e-blasts, etc.
- Create a YouTube channel for the library and recruit your Teen Advisory Group members to make brief ads promoting events. Link to them or embed them on the library's web site or Facebook page
- Leverage visual tools like Instagram and Vine to create quick but eye-catching promotions, or tap your Teen Advisory Group members to do so

IN THE PUBLIC AND PRIVATE SCHOOLS AND TO HOMESCHOOLERS

- ask to have an article in the English department's newsletter
- post fliers on the faculty room's bulletin board
- send an article to the school newspaper
- send emails or letters to faculty members in appropriate subject areas asking them to encourage their students to participate
- send emails or letters to school librarian, asking for help in spreading the word
- for contests, display the winning entries at school (after they have been at the public library)
- offer to booktalk and make classroom visits
- have table at back to school events, to promote e-resources, homework assistance, college and career planning resources, and upcoming YA programs
- read announcements on the public address system, or send them a slide to use with their video announcements
- ask to make a PSA for the school radio station
- ask school librarian for suggestions of students to involve in your Teen Advisory Group

- post fliers in computer lab
- put a display in the case in school library or main hallway
- have fliers in school library media center, preferably at the circulation desk
- ask to be included in the summer events newsletter distributed at school
- give presentation about the library program and services at a homeschooling parents' meeting
- recruit storytellers and program aides in presentations to child development classes
- distribute program surveys to classes—ask what teens want and let them know what they've been missing!

EASY IDEAS FOR SCHOOL/PUBLIC COOPERATION

- Link to each other's web sites and follow each other on social media
- Attend each other's staff meetings periodically
- Add each other to your mailing lists
- Invite each other to your library events
- Promote each other's' programs/services in newsletters, on the web site, etc.
- Public library staff visit schools to promote summer reading/learning programs
- Schools share assignment information with public libraries
- Teachers and school librarians can be asked to volunteer for summer reading/learning programs at public libraries
- Public library staff attend open houses/back to school nights
- Data sharing on things like teen demographics to inform decision making

INTERMEDIATE ACTIVITIES TO COORDINATE

- Hosting regular book talking events
- Co-facilitating teen book groups
- Organizing public library card sign-up events at schools

- Implementing joint programming, such as Teen Read Week™ events
- Reviewing materials together and sharing copies of books
- Putting together special collections for assignments
- Organizing tutoring or homework help programs
- Schools share summer reading lists with public libraries in advance
- Host a twice a year materials review session to exchange information about new library resources and plan strategically for future purchases
- Work together to bring in authors or other speakers and share the cost
- Influencing administrators on the importance of collaboration
- Do a job shadow day at each other's library to learn what their key needs and responsibilities are
- Co-creating resource packets for parents and caregivers
- Identifying and reaching out to youth serving organizations in the community to exchange information and

CHALLENGING ACTIVITIES TO COORDINATE

- Co-planning and conducting workshops to train teachers/school librarians
- Making joint purchases for the collections
- Sharing the same online catalog
- Seeking grants together to support a joint project

HOW TO GET YOURSELF INVITED?

- Start with personal connection: send an email to an individual and follow up with a phone call at a time of day that won't be too busy
- Have something of use to offer them – don't just ask for something for your library
- Don't try to schedule yourself for first staff meeting of the year
- Take any time offered and don't go over time
- Public libraries should start with the school librarian, but get your foot in the door anywhere and build from there. Other possibilities:
  o English department faculty
  o PTA/PTO groups
  o Afterschool clubs
  o Guidance counselors
- School library staff should start with whichever public library staff serve teens. Titles could be: teen services librarian, youth librarian, children's librarian or something else. Other possibilities:
  o Outreach librarian
  o Friends of the Library groups
  o Library director

Appendix H

Programming Around National Celebrations & Events

HERE ARE SOME major youth-focused events that you may want to celebrate in your library. The organizations that host these events typically provide free, ready-to-use resources from their web site that you can use in your library.

	Event	Date
Jan	• ALA's Youth Media Awards are announced at their Midwinter Meeting (awards include: Alex, Belpre, Edwards, King, Newbery, Printz and more). www.ala.org/yma. All of YALSA's annual selected lists are also announced. www.ala.org/yalsa/booklists	• Varies; announcement is on the Monday of the Meeting
Feb	• Library Lovers' Month www.librarysupport.net/librarylovers/index.html • Digital Learning Day, www.digitallearningday.org/	• All month • Varies

	Event	Date
Mar	• Read Across America www.nea.org/readacross • Teen Tech Week, www. ala.org/teentechweek	• March 2 • 2nd week of March
Apr	• School Library Month www.ala.org/aasl/slm • National Poetry Month www.poets.org • National Library Week www.ala.org/ala/pio/ natlibraryweek/nlw.htm • Celebrate Young Adult Literature Day www.ala. org/yalsa o YALSA's Teens' Top Ten nominations are announced (teens can read the books all summer then vote on their favorites during Teen Read Week) www.ala. org/yalsa/booklists	• All month • All month • Varies • Thurs. of Natl. Library Week
May	• Latino Books Month www.publishers.org/ • Free Comic Book Day www.freecomicbookday. com	• All month • Varies, but always during the 1st week

	Event	Date
June	• Audiobooks Month, www.audiopub.org/ events-jiabm.asp • GLBT Book Month • National Summer Learning Day, www. summerlearning. org/?page=summer_ learning_day • Make Summer, www. makesummer.org/	• Varies. Usually the 3rd week of June • Runs most of the summer
July	• Maker Party, https://party. webmaker.org/	• Runs most of the summer into Sept.
Aug	• Maker Party, https://party. webmaker.org/	• Runs most of the summer into Sept.
Sept	• Library Card Sign-up Month www.ala.org/ librarycardsignup • International Literacy Day www.unesco.org/new/ en/unesco/events/prizes- and-celebrations/celebra- tions/international-days/ literacy-day/ • Banned Books Week, www.ala.org/bbooks • Banned Websites Aware- ness Day, www.ala.org/ aasl/bwad	• All month • Sept. 8 • Last week of Sept. each year • Sept. 30

	Event	Date
Oct.	• National Book Month www.nationalbook.org/ • Teen Read Weekä www.ala.org/teenread • Lights on Afterschool, www.afterschoolalliance.org/loa.cfm • International School Library Day www.iasl-online.org/events/islm/	• All month • 3rd week of Oct. • Usually during the 3rd week • Varies, but held during last week of the month
Nov.	• International Games Day, http://igd.ala.org/	• Date varies
Dec.	• DeSTEMber, www.girlstart.org/our-programs/destember • Hour of Code, http://hourofcode.com/us	• All month • Usually second week of Dec.

Other resources to consult for calendars and lists of events:
- ALA's list of library events: www.ala.org/conferencesevents/celebrationweeks (focuses on ALA sponsored events)
- Follett Library Resources: www.titlewave.com/intro/calendar.html (lists literature focused events and some author birthdays)
- *School Library Media Activities Monthly's* Activities Almanac http://schoollibrarymonthly.com/almanacs/ (comprehensive list of monthly, weekly and daily celebrations and birthdays)

Appendix I

Seven Development Needs of Young Adolescents

I

1. Physical Activity

Young adolescents' spurts of boundless energy are as well-known as their periods of dreamy lethargy. They need time to stretch, wiggle, and exercise rapidly growing bodies; they also need time to relax. Adults who work with young adolescents need to remember the diversity in strength, dexterity, and size of youth in this age group. Intensity competitive physical activity often places an unnecessary burden on late bloomers who cannot compete successfully. Early bloomers who are pressed into conforming to sexual stereotypes that reward athletic prowess rather than on intellectual or social development also can be harmed by stressful sports competition.

2. Competence and Achievement

Because young adolescents experience extraordinary self-consciousness about their own new selves and the attitude of others towards them, it is easy to understand their overwhelming desire to do something well and to receive admiration for achievement. Young people hunger for chances to prove themselves, especially in ways that are rewarding if all goes well and not devastating if there are some disappointments. Young adolescents need to know that what they do is valued by others whom they respect.

3. Self-Definition

Rapidly changing bodies and minds require time to absorb new ways of thinking, new mirrored reflections, and new reactions from others. To accommodate the new selves that they are becoming, young adolescents need chances to consider what it means to be a man or woman and to

209

belong to a racial or ethnic group. They need time to find a friend and share a secret, or to have a good talk with an adult. They need opportunities to explore their widening world and to reflect upon the meaning of new experiences, so that they can begin to consider themselves not just as observers, but as participants in society.

4. Creative Expression

Opportunities to express creatively their new feelings, interest abilities, and thoughts help young adolescents to understand and accept the new people they are becoming. Performing and being exposed to drama, literature and musical works of others helps them see that people before them have felt the emotions and thought the ideas that are new and confusing to them. In addition to the arts, young adolescents can find opportunities for creative expression in sports such as synchronized swimming and roller skating and in activities like tending a garden or painting a wall mural.

5. Positive Social Interactions with Peers and Adults

Young adolescents' parents and families remain of primary importance in setting values and giving affection. Their peers offer needed support, companionship, and criticism. In addition, adults other than parents have an effect on the lives of young adolescents, who are so eager to understand the possibilities of adulthood. Young Adolescents need relationships with adults who are willing to share their own experiences, views and feelings with young people. These adults will also encourage young adolescents to develop positive relationships with peers.

6. Structure and Clear Limits

Young adolescents live in a society of rules, and they want to know and understand their own limits within that system. Clear expectations are crucial to unsure, self-critical young people. Their search for security in a world of conflicting demands is helped by explicit boundaries that define the areas in which they may legitimately seek freedom to explore. They differ from younger children, though, in that they are increasingly capable of participating with adults in framing their own rules and limits.

7. Meaningful Participation

Youth need to participate in the activities that shape their lives. Successful events are planned with, not for, young adolescents. As they develop a mature appearance and more sophisticated social and intellectual skills, they want opportunities to use their new talents. And, by learning that their actions can affect the world around them, they gain a sense of responsibility. Adults can help young adolescents see themselves as citizens by providing opportunities for them to make meaningful contributions to their communities. Adults need to adapt responsibilities to the short-term attention span characteristics of early adolescents, and to select varied tasks that enlist diverse interests and abilities.

Developmental diversity is the central characteristics of early adolescents. Because of the wide variations in "normal" growth rates during puberty, there may be a six-to eight-year span in physical development among any group of young adolescents of the same chronological age. Just as important, young adolescents mature at very different rates the new cognitive skills that begin during this time. A group of 13- or 14-year olds would probably include some girls who look like young women and are capable of bearing children. Beside these girls might stand girls who are just beginning to develop womanly curves and are not menstruating. A few boys in the group might look like strapping young men while others have barely begun their growth spurt. A few of the boys and girls maybe have mastered the new thinking of childhood and the abstract thinking that is more characteristics of adulthood. Because of their enormous developmental diversity, young adolescents require a variety of types and levels of activities designed to meet the seven needs listed above. Racial, ethnic, and gender differences among young adolescents require special sensitivity from youth workers. As young adolescents begin to consider what it means to be a man or woman and an adult member of an ethnic or racial group, they frequently identify strongly and exclusively with groups and people like themselves. They need experiences that affirm and strengthen their identification with their racial, ethnic, and gender group and make them feel good about being a part of that group. At the same time, they need experiences that gently challenge stereotypes of their own and of other racial, ethnic, and gender groups. They need adult role models who care about them and whose lives show them what they can become.

J

Programming for Young Adults, Based on Their Needs and Interests

"Because of their enormous developmental diversity, young adolescents require a variety of types and levels of activities designed to meet their needs."

[Gayle Dorman, "Seven Developmental Needs of Young Adults" from Planning Programs for Adolescents. Reproduced in The Basic Young Adult Services Handbook: A Programming and Training Manual (Youth Services Section, New York Library Association, 1997), p.195-196.]

Developmental Needs	Program Possibilities	Interests (what teens prefer to be doing)[g]	Program Possibilities
Physical Activity Boundless energy vs. lethargy Rapidly growing bodies Athletic competition can be stressful to late-bloomers	Young teen dances Fencing workshop Juggling Martial arts demonstration	Listen to FM radio (96%) Listen to CDs or tapes (95%)	Battle of the Bands competition "Win Your Favorite CD" Contest (gather input on music trends)

Developmental Needs	Program Possibilities	Interests (what teens prefer to be doing)[a]	Program Possibilities
Creative Expression Express thoughts, feelings, and interests creatively Accepting the new people they are becoming Exposure to arts shows that others have felt the same emotions new to YAs	Design & paint mural in YA area YAs present craft workshops for children Calligraphy workshop DIY and making workshops Create wear-able tech	Hang out with friends (88%) Going to parties (52%)	Poetry slam Comic Con event
Self-Definition need chances to explore ethnic and gender identity need time to share secrets reflect on new experiences participation in society	Cultural celebrations Career exploration Journal writing	Read magazines for pleasure (76%)	Establish a swap box for magazines and comics Editing a literary magazine or newsletter
Structure and Clear Limits Helped by explicit boundaries Testing limits Capable of working with adults to set own rules	YA Liaison to library's Board of Trustees Recruit teen interns	Watch movies (56%)	Lock-in movie marathon Make a music video workshop series Filmmaking class

Developmental Needs	Program Possibilities	Interests (what teens prefer to be doing)[g]	Program Possibilities
Positive Social Interactions with Peers and Adults Family primary importance for values peers offer support & criticism need relations with adults who share their feelings	Intergenerational book group Mentoring program Job shadowing program	Read books for pleasure (60%)	Make book trailers Write book reviews (publish on library's web site)
Meaningful Participation Opportunities for meaningful contributions to their community Varied tasks can enlist diverse interests and abilities	Young Adult Advisory Council (YAAC) Junior Friends of the Library group	Care for children (36%) Doing volunteer work (25%)	Babysitting classes Teen volunteers to assist children's summer reading program Teens lead children's story time Community service projects
Competence and Achievement Overwhelming desire to do something well Looking for admiration want chances to prove themselves, yet self-conscious want respect	"Tech Trainers" corps of tutors for one-on-one assistance to patrons Create web content for the library's site	Using a computer at home (64%) Using the Internet (44%)	Coding classes Gaming tournaments

About the Author

MEGAN P. FINK is a middle school librarian at Charlotte Country Day School. She began her career in children's book publishing, but fell in love with libraries while working for the New York Public Library. She is an active member of YALSA and has served on YALSA's Award for Excellence in Nonfiction for Young Adults, Teen Read Week and Best Books for Young Adults committees. Megan has written for VOYA, YALS and BOOKLINKS magazines.